EXPLORING THE BIG BEND COUNTRY

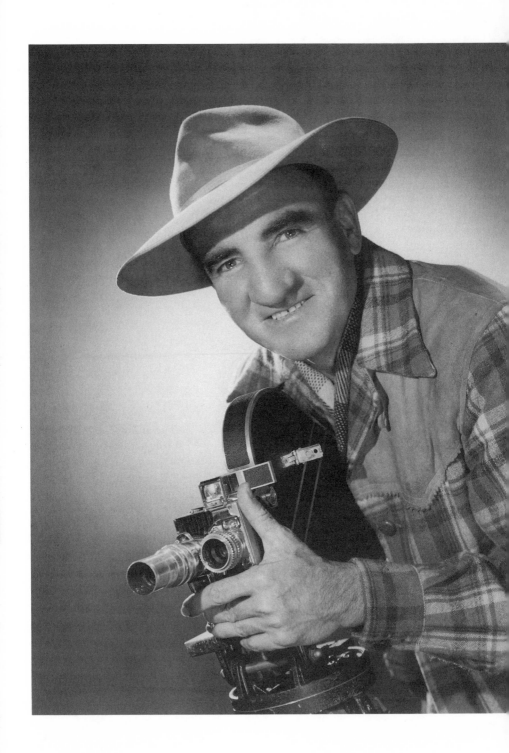

Exploring
THE BIG BEND
COUNTRY

PETER KOCH *and* JUNE COOPER PRICE

University of Texas Press
Austin

Requests for permission to reproduce material from this work should be sent to:
    Permissions
    University of Texas Press
    P.O. Box 7819
    Austin, TX 78713-7819
    www.utexas.edu/utpress/about/bpermission.html

∞ The paper used in this book meets the minimum requirements of ANSI/NISO Z39.48-1992 (R1997) (Permanence of Paper).

LIBRARY OF CONGRESS CATALOGING-IN-PUBLICATION DATA

Koch, Peter, 1904–1986.
Exploring the Big Bend Country / Peter Koch and June Cooper Price. — 1st ed.
    p. cm.
Includes bibliographical references and index.
    ISBN-13: 978-0-292-71654-4 (cloth : alk. paper)
    ISBN-10: 0-292-71654-0 (cloth : alk. paper)
    ISBN-13: 978-0-292-71655-1 (pbk. : alk. paper)
    ISBN-10: 0-292-71655-9 (pbk. : alk. paper)
    1. Natural history—Texas—Big Bend Region. 2. Big Bend Region (Tex.) I. Price,
June Cooper, 1933– II. Title.
    QH105.T4K63 2007
    508.764'93—dc22
                                                                2006028298

This book was compiled for Peter Koch's great-grandsons—Peter,
David, Chris, Ben, Austin, Steven, Alistair, Matthew, and Cole—and
his only great-granddaughter, Amanda.
You never had a chance to know him, or to hear the things he would
want you to know about the Big Bend.
Perhaps these words will bridge that gap.

It is also for all those who love the Big Bend Country.
The explorers, the photographers,
and those who see beyond the distant mountain ranges to a distant
time, a distant place, and a distant frame of mind.

A good photograph is knowing where to stand.

Ansel Adams

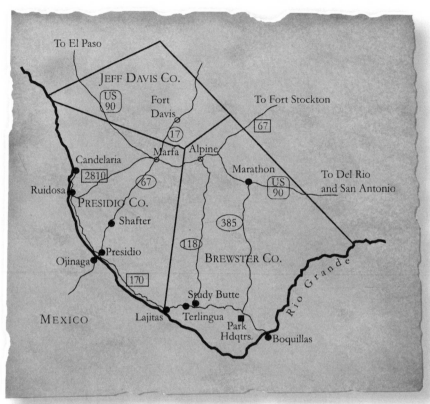

1. The Big Bend Country

CONTENTS

ILLUSTRATIONS

ACKNOWLEDGMENTS

FIRST, I WANT TO THANK MELLETA BELL and her staff at the Archives of the Big Bend, in Alpine, Texas. They have been custodians of the Peter Koch Photographic Collection since my father died in 1986. Their helpfulness and hospitality while I agonized over the selection of images for this book made every day a happy one. Michael Howard, digital imaging technologist, performed magic to repair many of the fifty-year-old photos I wanted to include. I know his work will meet the high expectations of the University of Texas Press.

At the University of Texas Press, I would like to thank Bill Bishel, Mary LaMotte, Kathy Bork, and others who contributed their time and talents to the production of this book.

I also want to thank my friend Mary Lynn Gilmour, who helped me page proof the final manuscript.

Friends and family contributing words and memories to this manuscript include Ross Burns, Betsy (Koch) Clark, Jimmie and Bill Cooper, Donald Dhonau, B. J. Gallego, Ted Gray, Celia and Rusty Hill, Patricia Koch, and Byron Smith. Their thoughts add the dimension I feel was needed to describe the unique life we lived in the early days of Big Bend National Park.

I also want to acknowledge the time Celia and Rusty Hill spent at their home in La Junta showing me how to build an ocotillo fence and picturesque garden walls. The unique creations consisting of discarded tires and aluminum cans neatly covered with concrete plaster. They are beautiful structures in tune with the desert landscape, in addition to being a delightful environmental solution that should be considered by all dwellers in the Southwest.

As always, I thank my husband, Marcus, for his patience and willingness to accompany me on our frequent trips to the Big Bend Country and for sharing his patience, expertise, and computer wisdom, which allowed this story to be written.

June Cooper Price

EXPLORING THE BIG BEND COUNTRY

INTRODUCTION

PETER KOCH (pronounced "coke") spent his lifetime climbing mountains. As soon as one summit was reached, he found another lofty goal to take its place. Well known in the 1950's for his lectures and his extensive knowledge of natural history and photography, he was also a positive thinker and a public speaker gifted with confidence and authority.

Peter Koch would have described himself only as a self-taught photographer interested in nature. He was thoughtful, focused, and I thought he could do just about anything, but, then, I was his oldest daughter.

Dad was strict but never negative. He taught us respect not only for people but also for the natural world he found so important. He also taught by deed, not word, and filled our home with classical music and literature purchased on his lecture tours.

Dad and his family arrived in the United States from Romania when he was nine. His first challenge must have been learning English and the customs of America. As a Boy Scout, he was introduced to photography and discovered his lifelong passion. His curiosity about the wildlife of this country is evident in his first simple negatives of flowers, birds, and butterflies.

This Introduction should also include a few words about our family as it was in our "life before Texas." Dad, my mother, Etta, and two younger sisters, Betsy and Patricia (Patti), completed my immediate family. We lived in the quiet rural community of Terrace Park, a few miles east of Cincinnati, Ohio. Dad provided a modest but comfortable living as chief photographer for the *Cincinnati Times-Star*. He was also associated with the Museum of Natural History and was occasionally an instructor of photography at the University of Cincinnati Evening College. However, even more important than his career was the enjoyment he found outdoors as a self-taught naturalist and a dedicated wildlife photographer.

I recall our comfortable, small white house in Terrace Park, surrounded by woods and fields. I enjoyed climbing the sycamore trees and playing house in the woods behind the garage. I was much too busy to be surprised the day Dad came home towing a twenty-three-foot house trailer behind his Chevrolet.

It was 1944 when Dad requested a leave of absence from the newspaper. My parents told me we were going to Arizona to see if the climate would cure my mother's asthma. Betsy was seven; Patti was almost two. I was eleven and ready for adventure.

Photographers were excited at this time about the high quality of Kodak's newly introduced color movie film. Dad was particularly interested in its potential to offer a more appealing presentation of his wildlife films. He called them "documentaries"—like those I'd seen when he took me to the Museum of Natural History on Saturday morning. He felt the quality of Kodak's movie film would be a big factor in launching a new career. Dad wanted to finish his two natural history films, which were already in progress, and planned to do another of the Arizona desert while Mom regained her health.

It was early in September of 1944 when Dad hooked up the trailer Mother had named "Porky the Road Hog." We crossed the Ohio River and headed for adventure.

We stopped first in Gatlinburg, Tennessee, to enjoy the fall colors while my father finished filming *Along Smoky Mountain Trails*. We spent the Christmas holiday in Venice, Louisiana, as he worked on final footage of the Mississippi River delta for *The Blue Goose Flies South*.

While we were in the Smoky Mountains, National Park Service officials asked him if he had time to swing by newly established Big Bend National Park, in southwestern Texas, and take photographs for their files. Dad accepted the assignment, and in February we crossed the Mississippi and followed the sunny skies to Texas.

Both my parents were thrilled by the rugged beauty of the Big Bend and the mysterious Chisos Mountains rising high above the surrounding desert. They parked our trailer in the Basin beneath the piñon pines at the foot of Casa Grande and decided we might as well spend the summer. Mother recovered her health in the clean western air and soon joined us as we hiked the mountain trails and walked the windswept desert filled with intriguing wildlife, incredibly thorny plants, and ancient history.

Dad was excited about the photographic possibilities of the country, so Mother was not surprised when he decided to do a documentary of the Big Bend. His new film was conceived while he climbed the mountains, explored the canyons, and walked the silent deserts. His keen perception of the country and a curiosity about its people grew swiftly. Before long, his thoughts of leaving the Big Bend vanished like a desert whirlwind.

Just where is this incredibly magic place? Look at a map of Texas and you will see, in the southwestern part of the state, an area that dips down into Mexico. The Rio Grande and the Río Conchos get credit for carving this exceptional "elbow" as they flow to the Gulf of Mexico. The area within the encircling elbow is known as the Big Bend Country of Texas.

Dad was forty, just a "pinch" under six feet tall, with the tanned complexion of an outdoorsman. He had strong features, a lean body, and walked straight, tall, and effortlessly. I never heard him complain about his health or the weather, or brag about his accomplishments. His love for nature was passionate, and he quickly soaked up the area like a desert absorbs a slow rain.

He was as tough and tireless as a longhorn steer. His only weakness seemed to be a penchant for coffee cake at bedtime and a stack of graham crackers dunked in milk or coffee after a long hike.

Perhaps the snacks gave him the energy he needed in 1945–1946 to produce two full-length documentaries focused on the Big Bend. His lecture brochure says his oral presentation "caught the spirit and tempo of the land and the easygoing confidence of frontier people." It also reflected his understanding of human nature, gained in contact with people during his years as a newspaper photographer.

My father's approach to photography can best be understood from his words in Chapter 1, as he contemplates the meaning of what he is seeing and how to express these feelings on film. Just as an artist doesn't discuss his artistic emotions with casual acquaintances, he declined to discuss his photography. Setting f-stops and shutter speeds came to him naturally. Depth of field was not a conscious decision. In the early days, if he was in doubt, he tried several variations, but it was not something he pondered. More important to him was finding a location to best portray his interpretation of each particular scene. In his words, "What I saw and how I felt seemed much more important than how I did it."

He rarely included people, buildings, or other man-made objects in his photos unless they had relevance. He felt that these dated the photo-graph, and he wanted his work to be timeless.

In planning his documentaries, he began by visualizing the script and planning the story he wished to tell. Then he spent weeks, sometimes months, searching for locations and symbols to illustrate his words. He introduced a poetic narration, which was presented in a masterly way, according to some who saw his films. It was a new concept, much differ-ent from the "incidental" style used by other lecturers. They would show a bird and name it, then show a flower and name it, and so on. Dad wrote the script as a story, then filmed scenes to illustrate it.

His film *Desert Gold* was extremely popular. It opens with a fast-moving sequence of Spanish explorers crossing the continent in search of treasure. He then tells an Apache Indian legend that explains how their vast desert domain and the Chisos Mountains were created. It con-tinues with the legendary tale of Chief Alsate, whose profile remains as a silhouette on Pulliam Ridge to be seen forever by anyone entering his Chisos Mountain hideaway from the north. The film closes with the romantic story of Pabla Blanca and her explanation of how giant whirl-winds form and why sand dunes are so beautiful at sunset.

My father's agent, Harold R. Peat, booked Dad's lecture tours throughout the northeastern and midwestern states. They were quite popular. Gregor Ziemer, educational director of New York City's Town Hall, considered *Desert Gold* "a travelogue film that has everything it should have—Poetry, Color, Symmetry, Symbolism, Drama."

Residents of Brewster County were also pleased with the film. Local photographer Glenn Burgess wrote an article for the *Alpine Avalanche* on May 2, 1952, that includes these words: "One-fifth of the entire popu-lation of Alpine turned out Monday evening to discover what Peter Koch, nationally known travel lecturer, considered the value of Desert Gold, West of the Pecos. They found out . . . and also realized that Koch, as leading salesman for the Big Bend National Park, was indeed a pot of gold at the end of the rainbow, and [is] one of the best assets this colorful part of the Southwest has."

Meanwhile, Mother's health continued to improve. To supplement the family income she took a secretarial position in 1946 with the National Park Service in Big Bend National Park, and our family moved from our trailer into a Park Service apartment in the renovated Civilian Conservation Corps (CCC) camp complex in the Basin.

After six long, weary winters of living on the road showing his films,

Dad decided to end his lecture tours and take on new challenges. It was
1951 when he applied for, and received, a concessions permit to open a
camera shop in the Basin. He advised tourists on trips and camera techniques and sold film and inexpensive point-and-shoot cameras from our
remodeled house trailer. The front room became an office; the kitchen
he converted into a darkroom. He arranged for the publication of a
tourist handbook, *A Guide for the Big Bend*, written by Helen Maxwell
and illustrated with his own excellent photographs. Dad also entertained
tourists at evening programs with his Big Bend color films and slide
shows. Talented naturalists in all fields of study were visiting the Big
Bend at the time and often sought his advice on how best to meet their
photographic goals. In *Wild America*, Roger Tory Peterson refers to Dad
as "one of those fabulous individualists one sometimes meets at outposts
such as this. Graceful in his stride as an Indian, and tireless . . . he
knows these lonely deserts, mountains, and river canyons as no one else
does."[1]

In 1955, my father moved his business from the park into Alpine and
assumed the office of vice president of the Highway 90 Association, a
developmental organization of small towns along U.S. Highway 90 in
West Texas. He helped the association in its efforts to lure more visitors
into the Big Bend Country. In 1958, he bought a local postcard distribu-
torship. Dad published over thirty of his own West Texas scenic photographic cards for the line. He kept businesses from Del Rio to Van
Horn stocked with his colorful cards and display racks as he traveled to
business meetings involving the Highway 90 Association and its agenda.

He sold the postcard business in 1962, when he accepted the position
as manager of the Alpine Chamber of Commerce. During his four years
with the chamber he was also involved with organizations such as the
Big Bend Development Committee, the International Good Neighbor
Commission, and Rotary International. Local journalists dubbed him
"the Big Bend's un-official press agent" and praised his efforts in bring-
ing tourists (and their dollars) to the Big Bend Country.

In the mid-1960's, my father was asked to do a promotional color
film with sound to publicize the urgent need to create the Big Thicket
National Preserve in East Texas. It was a long 550 mile drive across the
state for each of his filming sessions, but Dad believed in the mission:
protecting the unusual ecology of a small, pristine portion of the Big
Thicket from exploitation by the oil and timber industries. The film was
a success and helped achieve the desired results. The preserve was estab-

lished in January of 1967. Supreme Court Justice William O. Douglas was an ardent and vocal conservationist and a firm supporter of the Big Thicket project.

Douglas made several excursions to the Big Bend Country on his visits to Texas. He participated in float trips through the canyons and hiked into the desert backcountry to photograph beautiful Capote Falls. During one of Douglas's visits, Dad arranged for a horseback pack trip with Buck Newsome up to Boot Spring and the South Rim. From there they rode down the Blue Creek Canyon trail to the Wilson headquarters ranch house.

In *Farewell to Texas*, Douglas includes lengthy descriptions of his impressions and experiences in the Chisos Mountains, the canyons, and the Big Bend in general. The quotations and comments attributed to my father led me to a better understanding of Dad's environmental thoughts and ideas during the 1960's. Douglas's foreword is an eloquent acknowledgment of my father's help: "Peter Koch of Alpine made me see the Chihuahuan Desert in a new dimension, took me to the relic forests high in the Big Bend area, introduced me to the golden eagle and to the music of the canyon wren, showed me the slow magic of sunlight on colored cliffs, and helped me discover the warm hearts of the River People."[2]

In spite of my father's many obligations, he somehow found time to purchase and completely remodel an abandoned homestead on fifteen acres of land just west of the scenic town of Alpine. Dad and Mother lived there for many years, enjoying the picturesque, uncluttered view of Twin Peaks from their patio.

About this time, Dad bought a Linhoff camera and prepared for a new pictorial challenge. Harold Rickett of the New York Botanical Society had requested photographs of Texas wildflowers for the society's fourteen-volume *American Wildflowers*. Dad correlated this request with local botanist Dr. Barton Warnock's need for floral photography to be used in his publication of three important wildflower books of the Big Bend Country. Together the team of "Warnock and Koch" searched mountain and desert for many months to locate and photograph hundreds of flowering plants. (All of these books were published in the early 1970's.)

In 1971, Dad opened Koch Travel with the assistance of my sister Patti. It was Alpine's first travel agency, and he conducted photo safaris through the Big Bend Country. He also organized trips into Mexico on the newly completed Chihuahua al Pacífico railroad.

His Mexican photo safaris began in Ojinaga, Mexico (across the river from Presidio), and crossed the desert to Chihuahua City, Mexico. After a festive weekend in Chihuahua, participants were treated to four unforgettable days exploring the remote mountains and valleys of the Tarahumara Indian country and Copper Canyon, the greatest of all North American canyons. Most of the rail tours continued west through the Sierra Madre to Los Mochis and the photogenic village of Topolobampo on the Pacific coast.

My father also somehow found time to submit occasional articles about and photographs of the Big Bend to magazines and to work on other projects. One involved photography for Texas Tech University's development of the Texas Trails System.

In the mid-1970's and the early 1980's, Dad began sharing his desert adventures and environmental philosophy in the *Alpine Avalanche*. His weekly column was called "Exploring the Big Bend . . . with Peter Koch." He rarely documented his resources in these articles, since his knowledge was accumulated firsthand or gathered from thirty-five years of reading, conversation, and extensive exploration. He addressed his column to the local people as well as to visitors, photographers, and others interested in knowing more about the country. He wrote often and with passion, especially in the later years, urging his readers to share his deep concern for the environmental well-being of the Big Bend Country.

Dad stressed the need for preservation of the fragile environment. He felt that those who used the trails, explored the backcountry, and floated the Rio Grande were the ones who understood its values. These visitors were the ones who would develop a relationship with the land. Hopefully, they would also defend from overuse and exploitation the values found only in a true wilderness.

In 1977, my father moved into the desert. His hands were trembling and his eyesight was failing. Neither could be reconciled to good photography, so in his typically stoic way he packed his cameras away, built a modest home near Study Butte, and devoted his attention to archeological work being done in the Big Bend. Most of his last published words were devoted to sharing his understanding of the prehistoric people who came to southwestern Texas as early as ten thousand years ago. He also began outlining a fictional book about a paleo-Indian Jumano clan living in a primitive Big Bend. In May of 1981, at the Lajitas Gallery, he exhibited a retrospective of his work and sold many prints from his large collection of Big Bend photography.

Dad climbed his "final mountain" and found eternal rest on April 29, 1986.

It is hard for me to remember, or even imagine, my father living happily in a large city, dealing each day with the problems and concerns of a metropolitan lifestyle. It must have been a time filled with deadlines as he and his cameras pursued the famous, the politicians, the sports heroes, and the achievers. I am sure he documented disasters, floods, and fires at close range and brought to his readers the visuals of happiness, grief, and sorrow.

But that is not the story he would want me to tell. In these pages you will read about his forty-year relationship with the West Texas desert, his environmental concerns, and his interest in prehistoric peoples. This text has been distilled from the more than 150 newspaper columns written for the weekly *Alpine Avalanche* from 1975 to 1980, as well as from an unpublished manuscript of his first trip through Santa Elena Canyon in Big Bend. In addition, I have also read his collection of books and pondered his photographs. Most of his photos, journals, and correspondence files are now resting in the Archives of the Big Bend at Sul Ross State University in Alpine. It was there that I sorted and carefully considered more than twelve thousand slides, transparencies, and negatives in an effort to choose those he would want included in this book.

You will notice three places where I have added to Dad's writing by inserting endnotes and important recent discoveries that pertain to the subject.

While preparing this manuscript, I wanted to include more information about Peter Koch as a family man, so I added several stories I think you will enjoy. You will find them following Chapters 2, 6, 7, and 8.

My sister Betsy's two stories recall our early years in the park. They might help you understand a little of what we girls "endured" whenever we were called upon to accompany our father—the mountain man who could hike all day without water, climb cliffs, capture wildlife in his bare hands, and sleep anywhere!

My sister Patti writes about her experience with floodwater at Hot Springs in the park in 1953. For a different viewpoint, my cousin Don Dhonau sent me his memory of one night spent with Dad in the field.

In our first year in the park we always seemed to have an assortment of insects and other small creatures snoozing in glass bottles under the trailer waiting for Dad's inspiration or until the sun was right for their individual photographic session (after which they were returned to their environment). My goal has been to blend verbal pictures with his photographic images to preserve my father's vision of the Big Bend Country from 1945 to 1985.

I hope you enjoy and find much to learn about the Big Bend in the pages that follow.

June Cooper Price
June 2006

2. Big Bend National Park

Santa Elena Canyon

*G*o to the River.
Feel the flow of water
Know the flow of energy
See the flow of life
Go with the flow.

Frank Deckert, Three Steps to the Sky

IT WAS MUCH EASIER to build a boat of flower stems than to explain, so often, why I selected such unusual materials. I can only say that the material was at hand, my need for the boat was urgent, and the quickest way to acquire a boat in this remote spot west of the Pecos—in 1945—was to build it.

On the Chisos mountain slopes grew countless agave, or century, plants, and it seems to me I measured every dead stalk before finding two matched pairs of ten-foot flower stems six inches in diameter. Construction required trimming each dry stalk to uniform dimensions, then wiring each pair together and securely binding them to crossbars with many yards of baling wire. This held the stems in the general outline of a raft (Figs. 1.1–1.3).

The raft was christened *Broken Blossom.* I did not expect a great deal of buoyancy from four flower stems, especially when a milk can and bedroll were lashed into position on the fore and aft decks, so it was not surprising, when I took my place center aisle amidships, to find she

1.1. The Broken Blossom *was constructed mainly of century plant bloom stalks and baling wire. This photo was taken at Hot Springs, where the boat was taken for a test run prior to my trip through Santa Elena Canyon.*

1.2. Under the canvas deck is an inner tube to maintain constant flotation. Under the waterproof canvas is a five-gallon milk can in which cameras and film were stored. Behind the canvas seat are my sleeping bag and food in a waterproof bag. The raft was successfully used in all Big Bend canyons during the filming of the first documentary of Big Bend National Park on color film.

1.3. Century plant stalks such as these were used to make the Broken Blossom.

floated two inches below the surface of the water. This only proved that the *Broken Blossom* was not only a boat and raft but also a practical submarine, with my torso representing the conning tower, and the bottom half of me comfortably cool underwater on a hot day. The raft's purpose was to take me through Santa Elena Canyon to photograph its marvels for the first full-length color documentary film ever made of the Big Bend Country.

The Lajitas [pronounced "LaHEEtahs"] Trading Post is located on the Mexican border more than fifty dirt-road miles from the national park Basin. It was there, in one of our nation's largest frontier areas, that my first photographic exploration of the Big Bend Country of Texas began.

My one-man expedition to explore and photograph Santa Elena was attended by everyone within thirty miles of the Lajitas border crossing. There must have been ten people and the silence was formidable. Ten pairs of eyes measured, first, the *Broken Blossom*, then me, in obvious disbelief. I caught the words "poco loco," which undoubtedly expressed their unanimous opinion. This unflattering judgment, however, did not delay me in securing my bedroll, food bag, and the five-gallon milk can containing film and cameras to the deck.

I waved a restrained farewell to the ten as the *Broken Blossom* moved precariously toward the main channel of the Rio Grande. With decks awash, I was on my way toward Santa Elena Canyon, eleven miles downstream.

The Rio Grande has been called the "Great Excavator" by the learned, and many other, more colorful, names by those in closer contact; but generally speaking, the Rio Grande and the Border are synonymous in this part of the country. In this everyman's land there are the "wet" Mexicans on one side and the "wet" Americanos on the other. One is seeking to earn; the other, to spend. But I was taking a middle course in the Rio Grande. I guided the *Broken Blossom* into the swiftest water whenever possible, but, in the frequent pools—without a current—my progress was laboriously slow that first afternoon.

The Chihuahuan Desert's vast spaces, incredibly rugged mountains, and awesome limestone canyons represent but a few of the unusual features along this section of the Rio Grande. Most of the area within the bend of the river was set aside in 1944 as Big Bend National Park. Few people are aware of significant water in the Rio Grande, but seventy-five miles upstream from my put-in at Lajitas, the Río Conchos flows north out of the Sierra Madre of Mexico and empties into the Rio Grande. The villages of Presidio, in the United States, and Ojinaga, in Mexico, are located at this junction, which has been known for centuries as La Junta. A sizable river is produced by this merger.

Ross Maxwell, the first superintendent of Big Bend National Park, warned me to be alert for high water while on the river. He explained that, on occasion, raging floodwaters from distant mountain storms pour down this watershed. It would be disastrous to be caught unprepared, as there was no way to leave the canyon once it was entered. To back his point, Ross showed me the U.S. Boundary Commission report of 1856. It reported that men under the leadership of Lieutenant Michler, of the Corps of Topographical Engineers, on June 25, 1852, experienced danger-ous foaming rapids in one of the Big Bend "cañons." The floodwaters extended across the canyon from wall to wall:

> We had all retired to bed, when I was awakened by a roaring noise, which I supposed to be wind. . . . It was not wind, but water. . . . I had made the selection of my camp on a spot which I supposed secure from any possible inundation, but on stepping out of my blankets found myself knee-deep in water, which was rapidly rising. . . . As we advanced the water came up to the chin, and the soft ground under foot gave way. It was with the greatest difficulty we reached the hill with our . . . instruments and supplies.

In an earlier report dated 1852, Lieutenant Michler wrote:

> The flat-boat . . . ran square against the rocky walls, splintering and tearing away her entire front; such was the force of the blow that the crew were knocked flat on their backs. . . . The expert swimming of two of the men, both Mexicans, who had dashed into the current ere the sound of the crash had died away . . . seized her lines and she was landed on the end of a sand-bar which most providentially lay at the foot of the rapid; a few feet further, both men and boat would have been destroyed, and our all—provisions and ammunition— irrecoverably lost.[1]

The river's frequently violent passage is also the force which carves the series of magnificent canyons through mountains rising on both sides of the border. Even today, the high, steeply cut mudbanks are continuously being moved, deposited, and moved again.

About six miles below Lajitas, I guided the *Broken Blossom* toward a rocky shoreline and lodged her neatly between two large boulders. With Supt. Ross Maxwell's warning in mind, my campsite was carefully selected fifteen feet above the river on a smooth slab of cretaceous limestone. On the fringe of my camp was a life zone in which birds and other creatures were intensely active after their long midday siesta. The serious business of hunting food occupied each of them. I sat quietly in the growing darkness and watched the continuous show as each tenant lived its struggle for existence—eat or be eaten.

After dark the actors in Nature's night club took the stage. That night they were in excellent voice. Just as I began to relax in my bedroll, SPLAT! Suddenly I was stiff as a rocket at countdown! Nothing else is so alerting or sounds exactly like the unexpected slap of a beaver's tail on the water. I waited for another "splat" but heard only the leopard frogs at the edge of the shoreline. Their united concert in perfect rhythm dragged on and on. Then one of those puffed-up frogs slid off the beat. "SQUAWK squawk, SQUAWK squawk, squawk!" Instinct should have warned him that being conspicuous in Nature's world was a dangerous gamble. His offbeat sound was an overbid for attention, which marked his location and made him vulnerable! During the silence which followed his demise, I fell asleep.

The victory that next morning belonged decisively to the creatures bedded down millions of years ago in the cretaceous limestone beneath my bedroll. My sore muscles and aching bones would have been better served by stirring a cooking fire into action on the theory that, if for any reason you can't sleep, you may be hungry. At first light I did get up, and, while mesquite logs burned brightly, took a quick dip in the river.

That morning I should have noticed the glorious sunrise and the clean desert air scented with mesquite smoke, coffee, and my pan of frying bacon, but after the brutal night I was in no mood for the poetic in any sense.

Carefully, but without enthusiasm, I prepared the *Broken Blossom* for the day's journey. The milk can was securely fastened to the front deck, bedroll lashed in place behind the seat, and all too soon it was time to sit on that cold, submerged canvas seat. Slowly the *Broken Blossom* glided out of the shadows and into the meager warmth of an early morning sun. From the sound of rapids, not far below my overnight camp, it was obvious the white water ahead was going to be more difficult than any I had run the day before.

Minutes later, the *Broken Blossom* was poised momentarily on the crest of the boulder-strewn rapids. Recklessly I steered her down the steep pitch, paddling furiously to keep her in solid water, careful to stay clear of white-water froth and boulders. The water's twisting, churning force was too much for me. I was not even certain of a way to keep her pointing downstream. With a splash, the *Broken Blossom* plunged from a swirling flume into the roaring cataract. She lurched against a huge boulder, which spun us around. Now careening backwards, we took another long plunge. Then I felt a jolting crash against a house-sized boulder and cold water up to my chest! Slowly, the *Broken Blossom* came back to the surface, water pouring off the sides. A thrilling ride over undulating waves was followed by a half mile of swift water. I felt much better now that the first hazard had been successfully conquered.

At the next river bend, it was prudent to swing the *Broken Blossom* toward a sandbar and check every item on board, as well as the raft, for possible damage. All the wire fastenings had held, the milk can was still watertight, and only a single deep scar on the raft gave evidence of our rough passage.

Far downstream, before the curve of the riverbank hid him from view, a great blue heron, unaware of my drifting craft, preened his feathers in the warm sunshine. By this time I was comfortable again and enjoying a leisurely course close to a high riverbank under overhanging, graceful carrizo cane. As I rounded a curve the heron again came into view. He ceased his rigid posture and walked directly toward me with a stately stride, majestically taking possession of a large, flat rock under the cane, not fifty feet away. Immediately, the heron became interested in spearing minnows. Silently, I floated nearer and had almost reached him before he saw me. He rose on massive wings with a loud "quaw-eerrk."

The moment of action flashed through my mind again and again. To record such a picture would be a masterpiece. That particular heron would never again be caught off guard by the appearance of the *Broken Blossom*, but since one of these unusually wary birds had been fooled, perhaps others could be fooled as well. I made the necessary equipment adjustments to accommodate a camera placed in shooting position. On the *Broken Blossom*'s bow, there was an open center, or well, where two agave stalks curved in a boat-shaped arc. The well permitted me to stand on the river bottom with the *Broken Blossom* all about me. By leaning forward with my head and shoulders resting on the milk can, and with my hat pulled down to conceal my face, I could place my paddle through the well and scull easily in any direction without visibly alarming motions of the paddle. My camera was secured in a forward position so I could sight ahead by looking through the camera's viewfinder.

Downriver, a small flock of teal was busy feeding in backwater shallows. I drifted toward them. All was going well until the raft hung up on some boulders too far away for pictures. You should have seen their fright when I stood up. Birds are not very expressive creatures, but those ducks certainly mugged an excellent facsimile of fear. A half hour later I reached another pool. By staying close to the cane, there was a chance for a shot of a black phoebe. When more rocks blocked passage at the end of the cane, I chalked up another failure.

Suddenly, there was a cloud of dust and a terrific clatter on the river-bank above me. I immediately pulled close to the waist-high bank and stood up quickly, just in time to stare into the face of a bleating goat. This was the ultimate in grotesque contrasts, and it shocked every symbol of beauty from my mind. A moment later a young Mexican boy, following his goats along the riverbank, rounded the turn. He was far more astonished than I at our encounter and quickly slipped back into the river cane.

In the warmth of a ten o'clock sun, I finally approached the deep slash in the mountain which represented Santa Elena Canyon's upper portal. At this point the river was squeezed down to fifty yards in width, and the *Broken Blossom* floated swiftly into the shaded enclosure between the two towering rock walls. I had reached the point of no return. From this point on there was only one way out of the steep-walled canyon, and it was seven miles downstream.

Overhead, the sky was reduced to a narrow blue ribbon. It seemed to rest on the converging walls of limestone. The sky seemed more important now that so little of it appeared above such an abundance of rock. The massive rock strata rose ever higher, layer upon layer, like foundations for the universe. The severe simplicity of this silent perpendicular world gripped me, and it took effort to recall the existence of the complex and the horizontal. Inconceivable at that moment were active civilizations and living forests, oceans, prairies, and deserts stretching into space horizontally.

Millions of years are represented in this canyon wall of rock—the remains of an era when giant reptiles roamed a vastly different earth as rulers of the land. It began in a time when life lifted itself out of the sea and stepped on a land not yet solid. Plants prepared a highway for this emergence, as they crept across the drying wilderness. Other eras followed, and finally Man appeared. Seeing such massive residues of death, he recognized how insignificant he was, facing the Eternal.

These thoughts were put aside as I continued downstream, frequently

1.4. The majestic sheer walls of Santa Elena Canyon rise a thousand feet above the Rio Grande.

careening into small whirlpools, which were thrilling in their constant circling but not dangerous. The main channel was easily gained by opposing the *Broken Blossom*'s inner side to the centrifugal current. This forced the *Broken Blossom* to the outer perimeter, where I could easily enter the downstream current. I raced from pool to riffle, paddling the raft vigorously to keep control by maintaining a speed greater than the Rio Grande's. There was time to study the canyon in places where I could float without attention to hazards, but even this was too fast, so, when a small gravel bar appeared against the shore, I landed (Fig. 1.4).

At last my feet were planted securely within the majesty of Santa Elena Canyon. I was not the first but certainly, in 1945, one of the few and perhaps the best equipped. Upon my superlative twenty-three-cent *Broken Blossom* were excellent cameras and color film. In my hands these intimate collaborators—with my guidance—could preserve images of what I saw. I had only to feel and understand their meaning.

But my experience as a naturalist photographer from Ohio had not prepared me for Santa Elena Canyon. Its mystique was overwhelming. It was impossible to resist reaching out to touch the lower canyon walls, which countless floods had ground and polished to a satiny finish.

The immense layers of strata were separated by material which was deeply eroded. This material was gouged so deeply that there was no evidence of a supporting layer. Into these deep crevices floodwater had wedged rocks—lucky stones—which gave the ridiculous impression of supporting the entire mountain. Much higher, in pockets of windblown and rainwashed accumulations, small plants and spiny cactuses grew bravely. They hugged the canyon wall tightly against the occasional devastating winds.

What might lie beyond the next turn and the mystery of more hazardous rapids ahead brought my thoughts back to the *Broken Blossom*.

About a mile and a half into the canyon, the walls widened around a confusion of limestone boulders at the base of an astounding rock pyramid, creating an almost impossible barrier. The mighty roar of churning water encompassed me, and even before it was entirely revealed, I knew this must be the fearsome Rock Slide. One of the lucky stones must have failed or, more likely, the canyon wall had been undercut and collapsed. House-sized segments had fallen into a Rio Grande which merely raised its voice and continued to grind away. Brilliant slanting rays of sunlight streamed down to illuminate the canyon. The columnar rimrock high above the river caught the sunlight in long streaks, like exclamation points of pride in its canyon creation.

I landed the *Broken Blossom* among the long, flat rocks at the river's edge and climbed the high sandbank to look back at the narrow gorge through which I had come. Even the narrow "canyons" between skyscrapers in New York City do not impart the same feeling of confinement that I found here.

In pools away from the mainstream, water was clear enough to see two huge catfish feeding. From above they had the appearance of cruising submarines and weighed no less than forty pounds—each.

The Rock Slide was named "Camp Misery" by Robert T. Hill on his exploratory mapping expedition in 1899 for the U.S. Geological Survey. These were the rocks Hill described as an almost impassable barrier. Geologist Hill and his men spent "three miserable days" carrying their heavy, flat-bottomed rowboats (thirteen feet long and three feet wide) over the pile of rocks as they mapped the rugged country along the Rio Grande between Presidio and Langtry, Texas.[2]

Other adventurers followed Hill and survived to describe their hair-raising experiences. The massive river boulders against which others had crashed and found grief, and even death, surrounded me.

The turbulent panorama of the Rock Slide was not what I had expected! Perched on the highest boulder, I studied the churning water as it was forced between the massive boulders. Certainly, there were more magnificent and awe-inspiring cataracts in many parts of the world. Many large western American rivers boast of more tumultuous and extensive rapids. Yet, aside from the danger, Santa Elena's Rock Slide, and pile of house-sized rocks, had such a unique appeal that I sat for an hour or more searching for its message.[3]

At last, returning to the *Broken Blossom* at the riverbank, I carried the entire outfit up the clean sandbank to the canyon wall. Between two large boulders there was room to build a cooking fire, and nearby flattened surfaces were handy for food and utensils. I spread my bedroll over boulders in the sun, secured the *Broken Blossom* against the canyon wall, and stored other equipment out of the way as I pondered the mysterious qualities about me. Finally, I came to two conclusions: first, I would camp here until I discovered a way to film the Rock Slide's powerful appeal; second, I was hungry and had better eat.

My food supply was not exactly abundant, so there was no problem in making decisions. From my supply of pancake mix enough was taken for three large biscuits. In the fireplace, on opposing sides, two tin cans were placed so that the rims were on the same level. In one can, water was boiled for coffee or tea; in the second, a freshly opened can of beef stew was heated. Securely placed on the cans' inner rims above the hot coals was my frying pan for biscuits. None of my cooking utensils had handles, since they are always in the way. A pair of pliers in my back pocket served instead. Except for a porcelain coffee mug and the usual cutlery, these bare necessities completed my cooking outfit.

Cooking consisted of keeping just enough hot coals around the containers to boil, bake, or fry and timing the process to finish in the order desired. Success came in having everything done to a turn; but usually it was more interesting. Fortunately, burnt biscuits could be scraped to the desired color. If they were hopelessly dark, an application of extra jam usually made them tasty.

When my camp above the Rock Slide was ready for the night, I climbed to a lookout at a point of rock that might lead to new impressions and understanding of the Rock Slide's character and its powerful effect on me. There, I found myself comparing this river's tempestuous rage to the feelings Bedrich Smetana expressed in his beautifully tranquil symphonic poem of central Europe's Moldau River [*Má vlast* (My Homeland, 1875)—Ed.].

In the middle of the night I awakened, either from the discomfort of sand in my bedroll or the chill wind blowing through the canyon. With blankets pulled snugly around me, I watched the moonlight creep slowly down the cliffs then rose reluctantly from my warm covers to stir the campfire. How primitive, how mysterious—how thrilling! Around me existed only the ancient elements—Water, Wind, Rock—and my flickering fire.

Below, the fricative sounds of fast water boiling in a frothing turmoil blended with the thunderous booming from the depths and echoed from the canyon walls. A large flock of chittering cliff swallows, nesting near the rimrock, appeared. These birds, shrill and restless, plunged with great speed toward the Rock Slide to feed on insects sucked into the downdraft. Again and again they swooped, each time returning abruptly to the rim. The birds with their swooping crescendo added an accent which challenged the river's booming symphonic theme.

Runoff from a heavy rain far upstream suddenly moved into the canyon. The river quickly rose one foot, then two. Sand and gravel, dislodged from the riverbed, began to slide, and the scraping sound was like that of a huge creature—a "river demon"—moving underwater toward the barrier. Boulders bumped along. Air pockets released from the boiling current increased its volume, and the booming tumult echoed from the cliffs.

The convulsions of the flooding river glistened in the moonlight. The constant repetition of the cliff swallows and the moaning of the wind aroused in me a peculiar kind of fear.

I suddenly understood why primitive man had populated his world with supernatural creatures and powerful deities which could destroy unless pacified. Early man had need for powerful gods who would favor him over his enemies.

Thoroughly chilled, I returned to my fire, stirred the ashes, and added firewood to the glowing embers. Then, crawling into my bedroll within the cheerful circle of firelight and clutching blankets tightly around me, I fell asleep.

Morning coffee and a stack of pancakes with strawberry jam for breakfast! Then two strips of bacon and another coffee to be finished— after chores—at my lookout on the point of rock. Luckily, the floodwater had subsided after its four-foot rise, and it was about time for the sun to touch the cold rimrock with its warm light.

Studying a peculiar blue lighting was my absorbing interest when a peregrine falcon plummeted past me with a rush of air ripping through vibrant feathers. His surprise must have been greater than mine, for as he passed above me, he made a sharp little poultry squawk of surprise. How undignified for a fierce hunter to squawk like a chicken! He made up for this by angry, repetitious screaming when he reached his perch on a high ledge on the opposite cliff. His screeching soon brought a mate to assist him in his conviction that I was an unwelcome intruder trespassing in their hunting domain. I had seen nothing here which could be considered game for the falcons, unless it might be an occasional small bird trapped in the canyon by these swift hunters.

After their departure, I returned to my study of the blue quality of light on the smooth limestone. It seemed even more vivid on the lower canyon walls and rocks. This suffusion of blue is usually noticeable at the point of infinity in a view, but here it was most obvious on nearer objects. Changing my position also changed the effect, so I walked close to one of these predominantly blue rocks and discovered a simple explanation. The brilliant blue sky was being reflected in varying intensities from surface to surface. Each smooth and rounded facet reflected a richly softened blue sky, rather like a hall of satiny mirrors.

The falcon returned at sundown while I was again at the point of rocks. Above the river, insects caught in the downdraft from the mesa overhead were concentrated in a small area just above the river, where they managed to make some headway in flight. Several long-eared bats flitted about, feeding in these concentrations. Their erratic flight brought them so close I felt the draft from their leathery wings. Again the rush of air and feathers! This time the falcon barely cleared the top of my head and, not fifty feet beyond with outstretched talons, hit the bat nearest me with such force there was an explosive "pop." Then, gliding upward with undiminished speed, the falcon bent forward to pierce the skull of the bat with his beak. Gripping his prey in one set of talons, he hovered at the apex of his flight, looked down at me defiantly, then swiftly winged away.

My study of the Rock Slide the next morning convinced me it was possible to navigate the *Broken Blossom* among the boulders and through the Rock Slide to rapids and the open water below. I double-checked all equipment fastenings and took a firm grip on the paddle. My route lay close to the American shore, along a wide arc where less-violent water would not crush the *Broken Blossom* under the pile of house-sized boulders or trap us in pockets from which there was no escape.

Carefully, I launched the craft. It poised momentarily on the first crest of the steep pitch through the boulder-strewn rapids. After an exciting few minutes in white water, and two sharp turns, I put all the power possible into my paddle. Luckily, we slid through a narrow opening between two boulders, across a pool, and then down a final steep plunge into the last swirling whirlpool. The "demon" of the Rock Slide had been vanquished!

Exhilarated, I parked the *Broken Blossom* on beam ends next to my gear, carried over the Rock Slide earlier. For the second time that morning I built a fire and huddled close, shivering with cold and excitement at the memory of my success. During the next three hours, with light at its best, I was busy clambering over boulders with movie and still cameras, looking for places likely to yield a permanent record of what I saw and felt. There were many limitations as to what could be done, and these were mostly my shortcomings, but the effort did not lack enthusiasm or hard work.

The larger cameras were finally stored in the milk can and the miniature fastened in my shoulder holster, and again I returned to the rapids. I was still trying to inject visible symbols for the river's unusual sound and the strange pattern of its tempo. In frustration, I returned to my campfire.

A slow, gentle rain began in the night. By morning the constant seepage marked the canyon walls with long, dark streaks below every cleft in the rimrock. The usual crisp dryness of the desert night was dissipated. Even my breakfast biscuits baked soggy as a sultry greenhouse atmosphere spread over the canyon country.

Predawn lighting on a mackerel sky was of that opalescent pink color so often seen in the Big Bend. Above the canyon walls the color seemed even more beautiful due to the complementary blue gray color of shaded canyon walls. My departure from the Rock Slide that morning was leisurely, and soon I was drifting downstream without effort through the narrowest portion of Santa Elena. There was no vegetation on the slick, water-polished shelves of limestone stair-stepping up from the river. Only the water and the towering canyon walls were visible. Only the downstream riffles of the Rio Grande could be heard. A mile below the Rock Slide, smoothly curved sand dunes finally appeared to soften the bleak appearance of the canyon's shoreline.

At a twist in the river, a canyon wren's ecstatic song, with its melodious descending scale, announced my arrival at an expansive new canyon world of green. Carrizo cane arched and swayed in the gentle breeze. Bermuda grass covered the canyon's sloping shoreline to a height of ten feet above the water. On higher slopes, above the grass, the night's soaking rain had expanded the dry, crumbling, brown resurrection plants into clumps of luxurious green leaves. Their quick regeneration was more phenomenal when thousands of them were seen crowding the north-facing slopes. Gone was the world of barren rock. The resurrection plants had performed a splendid miracle of transformation. Nearby, a tall pillar of rock leaned against the canyon wall, like a giant who had also stopped for a long look at the view. Above it all, the golden cliffs seemed to rise more majestically—reaching into a hazy blue sky.

On a thick mat of grass I hurriedly made camp. My exploration that day led me into a steep side canyon which widened into a natural amphitheater. At its center I came upon a quiet, crystal clear pool, sparkling in the sunlight, as clear and green as an emerald. Tall ferns crowded the water's edge and streamed up the limestone slope. Masses of maidenhair fern drooped from hanging gardens around the pool's edge. Not a leaf stirred. Reflected light from the emerald pool rippled across translucent green fronds—transfixed and silent. I had stepped into a rare garden of ferns in a desert wilderness. The suspense of its calm was exciting, breathtaking! I backed away as if I had entered a forbidden sanctuary.

The rest of the day was perfect for pictures. Available light added a quality of softness allowing penetration of detail in the shadows without burning out subtle highlights. I found nearly two dozen species of ferns and their relatives that day, hidden in side canyon pockets on both sides of the river. It seemed unbelievable that so many ferns had adapted themselves to this environment and had survived to represent an era that was ancient long before reptiles abandoned the sea.

Another surprise in magical Fern Canyon was the discovery of a number of mushrooms. They were survivors of an era when this country was a rain forest. Investigating further, I found fossil and petrified remnants of palms, redwoods, and other rain forest trees. Among these ancient plants, but still alive, were two species of land snails which hibernate during the driest seasons by sealing the opening of their shells with a material similar to cellophane. It is amazing that for millions of years these simple creatures have been manufacturing a substance which Man considers an achievement of twentieth-century scientific progress!

The green shorelines continued down the canyon for about a mile, then the slanting rock strata lifted the vegetated slopes from river level to a height of several hundred feet. At this point, an arching cave marks the canyon wall on the Mexican side. It is known locally as Smugglers Cave, or the Cattle Cave. During the days of Comanche raids, this cave was reportedly used as a livestock hideaway by the ranchers. Since raids were frequent and longhorn cattle, horses, and goats plentiful, there ought to be some evidence of that use. But after climbing the steep slope to the cave, I found nothing. It is not even a cave—simply a very shallow overhanging bluff.

The *Broken Blossom* carried me past ever higher canyon walls, at times rising abruptly from the river in a deeper, greater replica of the upper canyon. The rising slanted strata created the illusion of coasting down a steep hill of water. The current was enjoyable, required no effort, and at the same time permitted me to see, lying back against my bedroll, the thousand-foot elevation of the rimrock as it rose slowly to its greatest height. Soon, the sheer cliffs towered fifteen hundred feet above me and the muddy Rio Grande.

When the river curved without notice, a glimpse of willows and cottonwoods appeared in the brightness ahead. After six days of isolation, I was suddenly eager to leave this primeval world of rock and quickly set my camera to capture the first view of the vast, brilliant desert horizon. Never before had the sky seemed so clear, so bright, so welcome.

Then, as the raft rounded the final turn, a fellow standing on a massive boulder began yodeling lustily. The canyon walls echoed his "O-lay-dee-ooo, lay-ee-oo, lay-ee-ooo!"

The cliffs on the Mexican side re-echoed the joyful welcome—"Ole! Ole! Ole!"

MOUNTAIN TRAILS

On any hike in the Big Bend it is most important to let someone know where you are going and when you will return.

Peter Koch

AT THE YELLOW PINNACLES on Toll Mountain I walked as quietly as possible, hoping the jays and smaller birds would not call out in alarm, giving the white-tailed deer among the rocks and thickets at Boulder Meadow notice of an intruder. The air was very still and the noonday vista shimmered with heat. The only sound was my quickened heartbeat from the exertion of the climb. At a point above the boulders I eased off the trail and silently made my way down the slope, using each volcanic rock for cover and peering carefully around their edges to scout the area I would enter next. Boulder Meadow, because it is shaded during the hottest part of the day, is an excellent place to find white-tailed deer taking a midday siesta in their natural environment.[1]

That day a buck and his harem were working their way cautiously down the slope. I crouched comfortably and low beside a boulder, since it would be unwise to move position, however slightly, when the deer came closer. I watched them approach my location and made the necessary adjustments to my movie camera. When they were about fifty yards away, their ears and heads snapped upward to attention. Their nostrils searched the air for any danger. The buck moved forward, stopped, and stamped his hoof. He moved forward another step or two and stamped again. When all of them moved, I picked up a rock, and the next time he stamped I pounded the turf to equal the number of his stampings. This brought the group closer for a better look. Their curiosity had lured them to within forty feet when I pressed the exposure lever. The whirring sound of the movie camera brought them to quivering attention. Slowly they approached the sound to within thirty feet, giving me excellent footage.

I was still a newcomer to Texas and the Big Bend, filming my first Big Bend Technicolor travelogue when these events occurred in 1945, and I still had a lot to learn about the country.

There are many ways to describe the Big Bend. To some it is simply a "homeplace." Others might describe it as a "state of mind." Some call it "heaven"; others see it as far less. Artistic folks appreciate its beauty— and there are a few who cannot move past its remote emptiness and find not solitude but "haunting loneliness."

From the beginning, I considered the Big Bend a fascinating land of contrasts and variety. The Rio Grande flows at only two thousand feet in elevation. Sixteen miles away, the Chisos Mountain cluster rises to nearly eight thousand feet. The inner basin of the circular mountain mass is probably eight miles in diameter and lies at an altitude of about fifty-four hundred feet. A trail around the outside of the mountain range would be about fifty miles long (Fig. 2.1).

This "island in the sky" is completely surrounded by chaparral desert. The Chisos Mountains, because of this isolation factor, contain species of flora and fauna that are different from related ones elsewhere in the world. For this reason, the Big Bend in the 1940's became a new and important research center in the fields of geology, archeology, paleontology, botany, and ornithology. I felt privileged to be there at the beginning, learning from outstanding professionals.

A few ranchers still remained on park land, and they, too, shared with me—in their slow, laconic manner—their experiences and vision of the country. I realized there was much to learn, and I was eager to see, contemplate, and understand all of the wonders that surrounded me. I feel compelled to share this knowledge—and my love of the Big Bend— and hope that it will lead to your enjoyment as well.

Big Bend National Park was officially established June 12, 1944, when, according to John Jameson, the State Park Board was given land, money, and the power of eminent domain. The Big Bend Park Association raised money to buy land, and the state appropriated more money. The state owned 112,907 acres.[2]

My family and I arrived the following February. At the time of our

2.1. Taken from the side of Casa Grande, this photo shows the layout of Basin facilities. To the left is the concessions area. The road leads down the hill to the campground then on to an area that at one time was Bert Beckett's horse ride concession area.

arrival, the first five Park Service employees were living in the old tar paper Civilian Conservation Corps (CCC) barracks in the Basin. [The area is now the location of the Basin campground—Ed.]

The full-time Park Service management staff was small but perfectly equipped for their jobs. Dr. Ross A. Maxwell had been doing geological work in the park for several years and was an obvious choice for the superintendent's position. Chief clerk Harry Linder came from the regional Park Service office in Santa Fe to establish the records and files. Orin P. Senter transferred to Big Bend from Hot Springs National Park, in Arkansas, and took over ranger duties for the entire 700,000 acres. Upton Edwards, a carpenter from San Antonio, soon arrived to begin upgrading the CCC barracks into more comfortable lodging for the staff. Rancher Lloyd Wade was foreman until George Sholly arrived in 1946. Mrs. Wade took responsibility for keeping the stone cottages clean and ready for the scientists—or curious tourists—who arrived from time to time.

It was a primitive life for everyone, no electricity or telephone service. The once-a-week mail delivery meant a thirteen-mile drive to the Park Service mailbox on Tornillo Flat every Monday morning. Employees learned to live with potbelly heating stoves and kerosene refrigerators. Limited medical service was available in Marathon, eighty miles from the Basin. It took about two hours to get there—unless the creeks were "running," and then it might take twenty-four.

It was a small staff committed to an overwhelming job, but they welcomed me and my family. They helped in many ways to facilitate my travel during the years of wartime gas rationing by including me on their inspection trips and sharing the flavor of the land and the people that is essential to understanding. As I took the photographs the Park Service requested for park publicity and records, I was also able to begin my own motion picture travelogue of the Big Bend Country, entitled *Big Bend, Life in a Desert Wilderness*. Many people in the eastern states had never even heard of the newly established park, and I quickly became dedicated to introducing Texas' newest park and last frontier to people across the United States.

Many first-time visitors had never seen a frontier borderland where nothing but space lay on either side of the yellow-striped highway. They drove the roads and saw only the monotony of fence posts, barbed wire, and creosote bushes. John Van Dyke said, "There is something very restful about the horizontal line. Things that lie flat are at peace and the mind grows peaceful with them." I felt that peace, and my love for the country was immediate. My original plan to stay two weeks was altered to include the rest of my life.

The first seven months of our Big Bend experience were spent in the house trailer in which we arrived. It was set up for us near a water spigot not far from the area where the lodge and gift shop are now located. We had a lovely view of the Window from the porch of the old store and spent many evenings there waiting for the sunset and watching the deer drink from the rusty bucket below the dripping faucet.[3]

There had been a CCC camp in the Basin during the 1930's and the early 1940's, but it was abandoned before the Park Service took possession. The CCC was created during the depression to employ young unmarried men whose families were on relief. These young men were the ones who learned the skills to survey and build—with hand tools— the seven-mile road you traveled up Green Gulch and into the Basin.

The seventeen road culverts they built remain strong and sturdy. They also built many of the hiking trails and the rock cottage rentals in the Basin.

At times I cringe when someone mentions photography. The word is usually the preamble to a discussion of equipment with emphasis on dollars or technique, which in any art is the skeleton carrying the heart and the spirit. But for me, what I saw and how I felt seemed much more important than how I did it. Camera and film were the elements which preserved, through my guidance, the factual reality, the outward appearance, and, hopefully, the significance of what I saw.

In my early years as a photographer of the natural scene, I viewed picture possibilities in terms of the vista. As years went by, I began to see pictures in terms of the foreground and its revealing detail in small, even minute, elements, much as Joseph Muench did. Then by careful means I emphasized the middle ground to show ground color masses, shapes, and lines; or I used repetition and contrast tied to the foreground. The background was designed to stabilize the composition and provide the perspective of spaciousness. These, in general terms, are the essentials I used to improve my photo techniques. Sometimes I found it took as long to understand the significance of a scene as it did to understand the personality of certain people. I'd like to share my experiences, and explorations, in the park with you and suggest hikes or drives that will be interesting and helpful to your understanding of the area.

Laguna Meadow–Boot Spring–South Rim Hike

If you are staying at the concessions area or the Basin campground, take time to enjoy the many hiking trails. I prefer any trail—even those with loose rocks that slip and clatter underfoot—to a city's concrete sidewalks and gutters littered with cans, bottles, cartons, and other garbage. Unfortunately, part of our pristine wilderness is slowly becoming less of an Eden, but in the Big Bend you will find many trails that are beautifully maintained yet give you the feeling of isolation. One of the most popular is the trail to Laguna Meadow, Boot Spring, and the South Rim. It begins near the campground and winds upward past the concessions area into one of the largest forest segments in the park.

Several ranchers had livestock in the Chisos Mountains before the park was established. Byron Smith once lived up in the Laguna Meadow/Boot Spring area. He was hired at the ripe ol' age of fourteen

2.2. The environment of mountainous Texas and many parts of the corridor between the Rockies and the Sierra Madre are similar. Residents of these areas in modern times and the very earliest Stone Age hunters adopted similar lifestyles to surmount the problems of survival. The photo of Red Rocks at Blue Creek shows a scenic view of a typical area of this type in Big Bend National Park.

to trap panthers for Homer Wilson, who had built his headquarters at Blue Creek and his ranch house in Oak Creek Canyon down below the Window. Wilson kept sheep and goats up in the mountains, where there was plenty of good year-round grazing. Byron lived alone "on top"— with only his horse, bedroll, food supplies, panther traps, and a rifle—for about a year (Fig. 2.2).

"There was no shelter," he said.

> At first I just slept on the ground in a bedroll. Then I pulled some logs in and built a three-walled shelter about 3 feet tall. I put my bed tarp over the logs to keep the rain and snow out. It was pretty primitive, to say the least! I cooked on a campfire and got my water from Boot Spring. Trapped and killed about six panthers! No bear, but I did see bear sign once in a while.
>
> About every ten days I'd ride down [Blue Creek] to the ranch and

pack in more supplies. Beans, flour, lard, baking powder, salt and pepper and shells to kill deer for meat. I was the first trapper for Wilson to work up there and worked seven days a week from "can to can't"! There were times when I didn't see anyone for days at a time.[4]

The Laguna is a grassy meadow. At one time it was a shallow reservoir where runoff from Emory Peak and Ward Mountain was contained.

Years ago, when the park visitor count was about 25,000 per year, only a dozen or so hikers a week ventured to Laguna Meadow, Boot Spring, or the South Rim. It was not unusual to have birds light on nearby branches to inspect a hiker. In the bed of the creek, birds and small mammals continued drinking or bathing with no fear. Hawks and eagles were even less concerned about human presence.

Hikers sometimes returned to the Basin wide-eyed about their dramatic experience. I recall one hiker's adventure. As he climbed the trail he suddenly came upon a young panther cub. The panther ambled over to him and sniffed his shoe. The hiker froze in fear as the cub looked him over. Then it turned around, and peacefully departed. It would be nice if all panther experiences ended so happily.

If you are visiting in late April or May, walk slowly between Laguna Meadow and Boot Spring. You might see the Colima warbler nesting in the oak leaf litter. These rare birds gather here from nearby high mountain areas of West Texas and northern Mexico. They have chosen the remote elevations of the Chisos Mountains to breed and raise their young.

Roger Tory Peterson, the well-known birder, author, and artist, came to the Big Bend to see the Colima warbler. He failed to locate any and finally said, "Let's see if I can talk to them." After a few squeaks and trills a bird responded and sat on a branch not ten feet away. Peterson had the same results with the rare Lucifer hummingbird. It takes a lifetime in the field and keen observation to develop such skill.

Strong hikers might consider an overnight trip to the South Rim. I suggest eating a big meal at noon and taking a brown bag lunch with you for evening. Try this trip on a balmy night of the full moon in June, July, or August. Plan your arrival at the rim for about four o'clock in the afternoon. Often rain clouds will be forming, or rain falling, at several places in Mexico around the Fronteriza and Encantada Mountains. The clouds and rain will add additional interest to your photographs.

Be in a position shortly before sunset to record this vivid event. A telephoto lens should be used if you have one. The lack of a striking

2.3. On a clear day, the South Rim view is phenomenal. It is also worth a climb to the South Rim when the skies are clear and there will be a full moon. That way you can take sunset photos and walk back to the Basin in the moonlight.

foreground is the main reason pictures here are disappointing, so keep that in mind as you walk along the rim (Fig. 2.3). There is no guarantee a superior sunset will materialize, but the view alone is worth the effort.

Be sure to wait for the afterglow on the Sierra del Carmen shortly after the sunset fades away. At that time the mountains take on a glow which seems to come from the molten magma of inner earth.

Emory Peak

There is a magnificent view from the highest mountain in the Chisos, Emory Peak. This mountain was named in honor of Major William H. Emory, leader of the U.S. Boundary Survey, which was commissioned to survey the U.S./Mexican border in the early 1850's. Years ago, when the air was clear, it was possible to stand on Emory Peak and see a hundred miles into Mexico. From that height I could also see north beyond the Basin, to the Tornillo desert and Santiago Peak to Cathedral Mountain just south of Alpine. At times McDonald

Observatory, a hundred air miles away, was visible—a tiny white speck on the Davis Mountains horizon.

An interesting footnote. While on Emory Peak one day, taking in the spacious landscape, I almost missed seeing a throbbing lump of ladybugs, thousands of ladybugs clinging to a single boulder. Where did they all come from—and why here? Were they aroused by the same instincts that motivate the swarming of bees and butterflies, or the migration of birds. Had Emory Peak become the "Capistrano" for ladybugs? I have yet to learn the answer.

Another interesting area for photography is Ward Mountain (Figs. 2.4 and 2.5). From Laguna Meadow you can take the dim trail leading westward, along its flank, to the most surprising features of all the Chisos Mountains. Ward contains beautiful high meadows and scenic views toward the South Rim, Blue Creek, Burro Mesa, and Santa Elena. It also has sheer cliffs of spectacular dimensions and awesome canyons dropping from sloping hillsides. It is heavily vegetated with numerous

2.4. In the 1970's, all that remained of the piñon and juniper groves which grew on Ward Mountain were some ancient burned stumps and downed trees, such as the one beside Barton Warnock in this photograph. In the far distance is Lost Mine summit. To the left is Casa Grande and to the right is Emory Peak.

2.5. *This view of the Basin taken from Ward Mountain shows the access route up the scree to the top of the Casa Grande cliffs.*

rare plants and is an environment which might still contain species new to science.

Ward Mountain is seldom explored because, from the Basin, which most visitors and hikers use as a starting point, Ward seems to be the least interesting challenge. Not true! Ward is a massive mountain with distinctive features that set it apart from its neighbors. You will also find it is the perfect place from which to photograph Emory Peak.

Juniper Canyon Trail

In 1949, Bert Beckett, a local rancher, developed the first horse conces-sion operation in Big Bend National Park. One day he proposed a ride from Panther Junction around the side of Pummel Peak and then up lower Juniper Canyon into the Basin. My horsemanship left a lot to be desired but I agreed to go. Bert explained that the trail was the his-torical route to the park's highest elevations from the Glenn Springs area. Bert was thinking of it as an overnight extension for his popular South Rim trail ride (Fig. 2.6).

Much of the track was no problem for his trail-wise mules. It was not until we lost the trail at the crossing of a deep arroyo packed with boulders and laced with saplings and tree branches that I was ready to turn back. Bert said, "Naw, we can make it." We unsaddled the mules and Bert led the way to the first large boulder.

When it seemed he could go no farther, Bert, carrying the saddle, stooped low under the branches, turned, and called his mule. The mule went down on his front knees and inched forward. After Bert and the mule cleared several boulders I started through the barrier. I was taller than Bert so of necessity stooped lower, and I had difficulty holding the mule's reins as well as the heavy saddle as I picked my way through the barrier. My mule easily duplicated the action of Bert's and we finally cleared the entanglement and again found the trail. Bert laughed at my distress at having to carry the saddle. He explained that the saddle horn might have hooked on a branch, and the mule, in an effort to free itself, might have been hurt. He was not about to lose a good mule just to save a photographer a little discomfort.

Bert's most popular all-day horseback trip led from his Chisos Basin corral to the South Rim by way of Laguna Meadow and Boot Spring.

2.6. Horses mow the weeds as they graze in the concessions area prior to their transfer to the stable. Saddle horse manager Bert Beckett (left) confers with Supt. Ross Maxwell and concessions manager Jack Lewis.

At the South Rim lunch stop he would gather the dismounted riders and take them to the edge of the two hundred–foot cliff. There, he would remove his hat and introduce them to the view by saying, "Folks, you can look in any direction and see the day after tomorrow!" Then as the group stood in awe at the magnificent view before them, Bert would astound them by throwing his Stetson over the rim. It would disappear momentarily, only to return in the strong updraft of air which carried the hat back up the cliff. The last time he did this there was no updraft and Bert's Stetson sailed out into space. It landed hundreds of feet below the rimrock never to be seen again.

There is no longer a horse concession located in the Basin, but the twelve- to fourteen-mile round-trip South Rim Trail is still popular with hikers.

From Boot Spring (where Byron Smith had his camp), the South Rim trail is bordered by piñon pines and stunted oaks. Many small broad-leafed plants, ferns, lichens, and numerous creatures are at home in this high, cool elevation frequently moistened by rain and windblown clouds. As you approach the South Rim mesa a creek flows over solid igneous rock with occasional depressions holding pools of water. These pools attract an assortment of birds and mammals. Years ago I made frequent trips to these ponds, where several golden eagles bathed in the early morning.

The eagle surpasses all other birds with its majestic flight. One eagle in particular was very important to me. I named the bird Hercules. He became a member of the family after I discovered him, alone and hungry, in a cliffside nest north of Fort Davis, Texas. The youngster was frightened at my appearance, and although he was only about four days old and still covered in down, he fought fearlessly. I wrapped him securely in my jacket, lowered him by rope to the ground and took him home. It then became necessary to find food—such as jackrabbits and "roadkill"—to feed him. Teaching him to provide for his own food was quite a chore, as you can imagine (Fig. 2.7).

Success came the day he swiftly and silently glided from his perch for the jackrabbit I held. Before I was aware of his presence, he knocked me over. Then he hobbled off, turned, confronted me, and knocked me off my feet once more. The third time Hercules swooped in, he gripped my arm with his talons, nipped me with his beak, and took the jackrabbit for his own. It was a rather painful success—for me. The next day I took him to the top of Lone Peak, the small rock-strewn mountain in the center of the Basin. I threw the rabbit I had hidden there off the cliff. Hercules

2.7. *This golden eagle flight sequence was taken from frames used in my Big Bend movies. The eagle was raised by hand but never confined. When photographing predators, it is very important to preserve the wild appearance.*

immediately understood and sailed down to claim his trophy.

After a few weeks of practice he was not only catching his own food but was doing barrel rolls, loops, and teaching himself to fly upside down (a necessary part of the mating ritual of the adult bird). His wingspan at seven months was six feet seven inches. He had a proud appearance and a fine bearing and became the star performer in my second Big Bend movie, *Desert Gold*.

Area ranchers, members of the Big Bend Eagle Club, were probably upset over my rescue of the eaglet. They were of the opinion that eagles, coyotes, and other predators should be exterminated to protect livestock, especially newborn lambs. Some ranchers enjoyed killing the eagles for sport and ignored the fact that they were overstocking their pastures, and because of the drought, their sheep and goats were starving. In twelve years (1930–1942) preceding the establishment of the park, the game warden and a pilot, at the rancher's request, trapped, shot, or poisoned twenty-five hundred golden eagles.

In 1946, the Eagle Club announced in the Alpine newspaper that the pilot had eliminated 856 eagles and 209 coyotes. It also insisted that "eagles are numerous in this area now with losses to livestock correspondingly high."

I kept Hercules close to home in the Chisos Mountains, then took him with me that fall on my lecture tour. Somewhere in the Appalachian foothills he escaped from the car and found his own aerie far from the gun-happy hunters of Brewster County.

Pulliam Peak Trail

In January of 1947, a subzero cold wave and blizzard stopped Big Bend traffic. Park families living in the Basin were particularly hard hit. Water pipes froze and melted snow was the only source of water for several days. At the height of the blizzard, Harold Schaafsma reported for duty as district ranger. He later admitted he was tempted to turn around and head back to balmy California. It was fortunate for hundreds of visitors who came to the park that he remained. For two years, he explored every prominent mountain and canyon in the park and shared his experiences with park visitors at evening campfire lectures.

It was Harold who first told me of a hidden canyon in Green Gulch which led to the top of Pulliam Bluff. Check with a ranger for directions to the trail on the north side of Pulliam Mountain. The hike is

2.8. This outstanding Texas madrone tree beside the road in Green Gulch frames Casa Grande. Concentrations of this evergreen tree occur in the high country in Texas and the northern mountain ranges of Mexico.

only for the most experienced day hiker. No camping gear, just cameras, binoculars, and water—especially water—are recommended.

About halfway up the slope to the cliffs are a number of picturesque dead juniper snags. The junipers form an unusual frame for photos of the thunderheads that loom over Paint Gap and Grapevine Hills. If you get an early start, it is also possible to continue around Vernon Bailey Mountain to the Window pour off. There, a climb up the talus slopes into the Window will bring you back into the Basin. This hike will include all the wilderness, isolation, and challenge you can take in a day. Be sure to report your intention to the ranger on duty before undertaking this strenuous and difficult hike.

There are also fine scenic camera views toward Pulliam Peak from the road in Green Gulch. For an interesting foreground consider the Texas madrone (Fig. 2.8). The tree presents a beautiful frame for any Big

Bend mountain scene. Farther down Green Gulch, tall grasses and cactus provide foreground framing for backlighted views of Casa Grande and the two pointed unnamed peaks near the top of the pass. Check out the scenes toward Lost Mine Peak and distant Panther Peak before returning to your car.

Photographers will find that lighting, which is so important to any scenic composition, works to their advantage in Green Gulch. With good light on the mountains and a meaningful foreground—with middle distance somewhat subdued—all you need are a few clouds. If you are lucky you might also catch a scenic view with the light of a rising sun through morning mists. And don't forget to grab a sunset shot through the Window before you leave the park. Either would be an excellent trophy of your visit to Big Bend National Park.

Lost Mine Trail

The Lost Mine Trail is not only the most scenic but also the most popular and widely acclaimed of all Big Bend trails. The CCC boys constructed the Lost Mine Trail, and their excellent work is one reason the trail remains one of the best and most scenic in the park. You will find limited parking at the Panther Pass trailhead (Figs. 2.9 and 2.10).

At the point where Lost Mine trail tops out at the overlook, a dim path leads to the left, or northeast. It is not the "rockhoppers'" paradise it seems, for these rimrocks are most dangerous. They are honeycombed with fractures, and large chunks will break off at the slightest touch.

Lost Mine Ridge is without obstruction, so it is a good place for birders to watch for soaring raptors above the nearby mountains. Updrafts allow ravens, hawks, and the occasional eagle to exhibit aerial skill. It is excellent picture country (Fig. 2.11). In the fall and winter, clouds swirl in fantastic mares' tails against a sparkling blue sky. In midsummer a black cloud might roll over the peaks and catch you unprepared. The rain will drench you so completely there is no need to seek shelter, unless it be from the bolts of lightning exploding around you.

2.9. The Lost Mine Trail was planned and built by the Civilian Conservation Corps, headquartered in the Basin during the 1930's. It remains one of the best trails in Big Bend National Park. This location is a good place for birders to watch for soaring birds above the nearby mountains, where the updrafts allow ravens, hawks, and the occasional eagle to exhibit their aerial skill.

2.10. Etta Koch stands at the overlook on Lost Mine Trail. In the far distance are the mountains near Castolon. Toward the foreground is conical Elephant Tusk. You can also see the South Rim bluffs in the middle distance. Etta is looking toward Casa Grande and the Basin.

These violent summer storms also occur in the Basin, but on Lost Mine Peak they are much more dramatic. A storm unleashed in this wilderness will etch memories in your brain that will never vanish!

During July and August, thunderheads—black and ominous—boil above other desert mountains as well. Some clouds mushroom overhead only to disappear without a trace of rain. Others drop an avalanche of water so dense the rainfall assumes the greenish color of a rain spout as it floods the country with four to ten inches of water. When that happens every dusty depression becomes a lake and every creek a raging torrent. Tornillo and Terlingua creeks and every dry wash in between are flooded to carry off the rubble with a roar that nearly matches the earth-shaking thunder overhead.

2.11. Patti Koch sits on the rimrock looking toward Pulliam Mountain and upper Green Gulch. From this place on the rimrock, towering hundreds of feet above Green Gulch, Lost Mine Peak becomes progressively more rugged. It is excellent picture country, but extreme care must be used when prowling around the edge of cliffs for your pictures of pinnacles, chimneys, and sawtooth ridges.

In the early days, before bridges were built, a flooded crossing on the unpaved road to the park would halt all vehicles. The first folks to come placed a rock or stick at the edge of the floodwater. Those who followed joined in watching the makeshift water gauge and awaited the eventual lowering of the water level. New arrivals would ask hopefully, "Is it going down yet?"

Old-timers say it was much more fun to be stuck at crossings when there were fewer people in the country. It was the custom for first arrivals to build a fire and have coffee ready for those who followed. Before the creek ran out, neighbors had time to share stories of their concerns and accomplishments. Finally, a courageous rancher in a sturdy pickup would brave the crossing as the rest watched closely to see how the creek flow might have changed the channel, or where a boulder might be lodged. If all went well, one by one a parade of vehicles would venture slowly into the flow of thick chocolate-colored water and continue on their way.

Pine Canyon

Pine Canyon, with its limited forest of pine and an assortment of deciduous trees bordering the creek bed, lies just east of the Lost Mine Trail. Many believe Pine Canyon offers the most vivid contrasts in the Chisos Mountain scene.

In the early days, it was called Wade Canyon because Lloyd Wade lived there. I was told Lloyd had the first bathtub in the Chisos Mountains. Apparently, he and his mules hauled it from town in a wagon, and I understand he had quite a challenge getting it up the canyon to his homestead.

But Pine Canyon is now known for its relic pine forest, rare plants, and, for most of the year, a trickling stream of clear, cold water. The upper section of the creek continues for several hundred yards to the pour off. There it lunges in a spectacular cascade down a scarp into lower Pine Canyon. Seen from below, the cascade at the pour off is the most beautiful waterfall in the Chisos. It is always worth a trip after the summer rains to photograph its misty fifty- to seventy-five-foot plunge into a rocky pool. Around the perimeter of the pool numerous long-spurred columbines and other flowering plants decorate a natural rock garden. The columbine is a Mexican species that occurs only in this area of the United States.

Undisturbed, and rarely visited, Pine Canyon is one of the best examples of forested wilderness. It is quite small but still conveys the mood of a cathedral forest. Roger Tory Peterson said he would rate his trip to Pine Canyon among the most interesting he experienced in the Big Bend.

Kibbey Springs

There are many levels of hikers. If your major effort is confined to surviving the unaccustomed altitude, try the level trail from Panther Pass to Kibbey Springs, midway up the slope of Casa Grande. The spring seeps a limited supply of water, and large boulders nearby provide cover for panthers, deer, foxes, ringtails, and weasels.

Once, while wandering the high country between Kibbey Springs and Toll Mountain, I saw a panther carrying food silently make its way down a cliff. This could only mean that young were in a nearby cave. The next day I found a way to the ledge on which the cave was located, and sure enough there were two tiny balls of fur hidden in a dark niche. I quickly crawled out of the cave and along the narrow ledge so my scent would not cause the adults to abandon the young. My intention was to photograph them when they were old enough to play in the sunshine at the mouth of the cave. The rest of the day I spent looking for a location on the opposite side of the canyon for a blind where I could, with a tele- photo lens, secure color photos and a movie sequence of the adults with their young.

I hiked to the location of my blind every day for more than a week but failed to see the mature panthers again. Perhaps the old ones had moved the young to another location. The only way to find out was to climb to the ledge and again crawl into the cave. Halfway to the cave the ledge broke and dumped me into a mesquite tree about ten feet below. I suffered three cracked ribs, numerous punctures and scratches from mesquite thorns, and, more regrettable, I had to give up the project.

Spectacular weather contrasts occur during Big Bend winters. It is true some discomfort may be experienced when a "blue norther" strikes and finds people unprepared for the fifty- or sixty-degree drop in tempera- ture—in a few hours.

Photographers should consider themselves fortunate if they are on hiking trails such as Lost Mine, Laguna, or Boot Canyon in the early morning after a four- to six-inch snowfall.

Picture a trail winding among the piñon pines. Long, thin icicles hang below the deep green pine needles. Pure white snow, in pine branch hammocks, swings gently in the breeze, which slides softly up the mountain slopes. The tinkling of icicles touching lightly is like the music of fairy bells. Hoarfrost coats every tree, bush, and cactus plant (Fig. 2.12). Century plants heavily coated with ice from this frozen cloud stand rigid against a vibrant blue sky. Soon the early morning sun rises over the distant ridge to highlight the snow and ice a bright iridescent pink. As the sun transforms the world into a sparkling array of snow crystals, brilliant flashes of light reflecting from the icicles have the fire of countless diamonds. You, the photographer, must work fast or the warm sun will have the forest of icicles falling down your neck as they melt and lose hold on the branches. It takes only an hour or so until all that is left is a thrilling memory and photographic souvenirs of a memo- rable day in a Big Bend winter wonderland.

2.12. A passing cloud has deposited an inches-thick layer of hoarfrost on the desert plants in the Chisos Mountain Basin framing a view of the Window. This is just another way nature emphasizes contrasts in the Big Bend Country.

DAD AND I HIKE IN THE CHISOS

by Betsy Koch Clark

I think I was in high school the day Dad suggested we climb over Pulliam Peak. We got in the car and went over to Green Gulch and parked it near the old corral and started hiking around Alsate and up a canyon not far from where we parked the car. The canyon was steep and we had mighty rough travel. Water had washed away the topsoil, leaving bedrock, but in some places loose shale played havoc with our footing.

I did lose my footing high up in the canyon and slid down eight or ten feet right into a prickly pear cactus—which I was thankful for, because it kept me from going all the way down. My knees hurt all day from the stickers stuck in my jeans. This was one time that Daddy had to come rescue me. He pulled me back so I could get up and very tenderly told me to be careful. I was glad when we topped out. There were lots of flowers and trees and it was very cool up there. But the sun had already taken its toll coming up and I developed a horrible headache. "Mind over matter" entered my thoughts and I didn't say anything for a while. We did stop, and he photographed the ferns or flowers, or whatever they were, up there, which was his mission.

I was just glad to sit down while I upchucked. It was terrible tasting stuff, and we had no water. So he told me to get some grass and chew the tender stalks until I could carry on. He waited patiently for me to gather myself.

When we started out again down to the Basin side of Pulliam— and home—I realized that my headache was gone. But I didn't feel all that great for the rest of the day. He was one tough hiker and knew a lot of secrets that I think about even today. Here are a few that come to mind. You might find them useful too:

1. Don't step on anything if you can step over it.
2. Hold your arms up to shield your face when going through thick brush.
3. Be sure and plant your foot before you put your weight on it when on loose ground.
4. Always keep your knees bent when coming down a slope— especially if it's loose gravel or a rockslide.
5. Don't sit down to rest unless you are taking a lengthy break. It's better to just chug along slowly. (And never wear new shoes.)

FORT DAVIS AND
THE SCENIC LOOP

*T*ravelers to the frontier military post of Fort
Davis have long been struck speechless by the area's magnificent vistas.

Gene Fowler

BACK IN 1849 the only road between San Antonio and El Paso was
considered a "highway of horrors" to those who had to make the five
hundred–mile journey.

West of the Pecos River, at the northern edge of the Big Bend
Country, the road to California crossed many miles held at the time by
the Comanche and Apache Indians. Swarms of settlers and gold seekers
were moving west, and they wanted and needed military escorts to protect them as they crossed the untamed Texas frontier.

Military surveyors Lt. William H. C. Whiting and William F.
Smith were the first to attempt a solution in 1849. Their reconnaissance
west of the Pecos is an interesting story.

The surveyors were escorted by nine Texas frontiersmen and two
Mexican interpreters, all under the leadership of an experienced guide
named Richard Howard. They followed the old road (from San Antonio) for many miles without incident, but as they entered Limpia
Canyon in the Davis Mountains their party was surrounded by two
hundred Mescalero Apaches, who came charging from the side canyons
brandishing their lances and strung bows. While Whiting and Howard
parleyed with the Indian leaders, the other men quietly moved to an ele-
vated defense position where they could "fight to the finish." The warriors grew less belligerent when they saw the Texans stuff their mouths
with bullets and cock their rifles. Not willing to press the issue, the Indians backed away and allowed the troops to continue down Limpia
Creek.

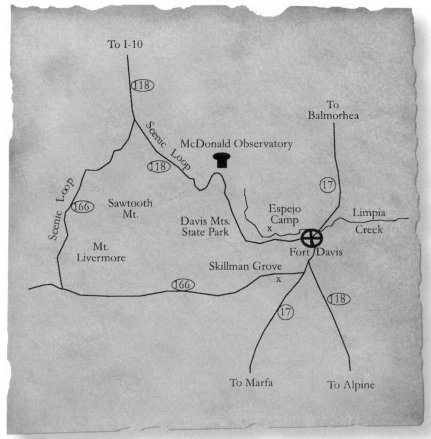

3. Jeff Davis County

Months later, after scouting an alternate route along the Rio Grande to the south, the soldiers returned to Limpia Creek. Their report gives some idea of the camp the Apaches established in their absence:

At first the bluffs on the right and left looked natural, then appeared the tall cottonwood groves, the first we had seen since leaving the Rio Grande. Doubts were at length removed by our coming to the "Painted Trees." But how changed from the fresh, green, quiet spot we had left . . .

To be sure it was as still, but the grass had been trampled by hundreds of horses. More than two hundred lodges had been placed around the site of our former campfires. Their frames met the eye in every direction. The whole force of Gomez' Apache bands had been gathered here, called in by the signal fires.

The collection of Comanche paintings had received some rich additions of Apache design. Some crudely done in charcoal represented Indians on horseback at the pleasant pastime of lancing ourselves on mules, and one which roughly portrayed our running away [which] aroused the ire of some of my Texans. Entering now the Wild Rose Pass, we soon halted for the night about a mile below the Painted Camp.[1]

In October 1854, the first military wagon train of construction materials made its way from San Antonio to Limpia Canyon and the "Painted Camp," which is known today as Fort Davis. It was Lt. Col. Washington Seawell, of the 8th Mounted Infantry, who directed construction of crude buildings at Fort Davis, the first military post in Texas west of the Pecos River.

Five years later, Lt. Edward L. Hartz left Fort Stockton with fifty soldiers, stockmen, mules, horses, and twenty-three camels. They had provisions for thirty-three days in the field. Hartz was an old campaigner, stationed at Fort Davis, who had led frequent patrols into the unknown and unmapped areas between Fort Davis and the Rio Grande.

Hartz's military objective in the midsummer desert heat of 1859 was to test the performance of camels on a variety of terrains and compare their efficiency with that of mules and horses. Lt. William H. Echols, of the Topographical Corps, accompanied him. Echols's mission was to map the area traveled and indicate the well-defined and hard-packed Comanche Trail, which led southward from Fort Stockton past present-day Marathon and on into Mexico.

South of Marathon the simple markings on the Echols map indicated elevations, ridges, and mountains but not the character or form of the area mapped. It seems likely, however, that the Hartz trail generally paralleled the McKinney Hills and a route along the west side of Tornillo Creek, ultimately reaching the Rio Grande.

On July 14, Hartz reported that "a rougher, more rocky, rugged country, can scarcely be imagined. Descending by very steep slopes into the beds of ravines, tumbling about for a while among rocks in their beds, climbing their steep hillsides, forcing a way through thickets, and crossing an eminence of an unusual height, may be enumerated among the labors performed by the camels during this tedious day's march."

On July 17, he wrote, "Our train crossed in the course of the day, no less than fifty seven arroyos, some of them fifty to seventy feet in depth. . . . The patience, endurance and steadiness which characterize the performance of the camels during this march is beyond praise, and when compared with the jaded and distressed appearance of the mules and horses established for them another point of superiority."[2]

The following summer, Lieutenant Echols returned to the Big Bend with thirty-one soldiers, twenty-five mules, and twenty camels for further mapping and exploration. His command was also charged with finding a suitable site and supply route for another military post.

The command nearly perished from lack of water sources as they crossed the desert between Camp Hudson on the Devils River and Fort Davis. Their report of July 2, 1860, reads in part: "[We] marched westwardly most of the day over rough country . . . camped dry without any prospects of finding water. We are all very uneasy, not to say a little frightened for our welfare. The mules must go without water tonight, are broken down now, and some are expected to be abandoned on the march tomorrow. Our march today has been rough. . . . I fear for the many lives that are now with us."

Two days later, on July 4, he wrote:

> The whole conversation was of "something to drink." We had to use
> our canteens as pillows to secure our water, as none of the most
> thirsty show much reluctance in emptying any one they may come
> across at a draught. . . . No one can imagine the feelings of a
> thirsty man, till he sees one. . . . I would not attempt to describe it
> by a vain attempt. . . . [Here] the scathing fire of destruction has
> swept with its rabid flame mountains, cañons, ravines, precipices,
> cactus, soapweed, intense reflection from the limestone cliffs, and
> almost every barrier that one can conceive of to make an impossibil-
> ity to progress.

In spite of the pessimistic report, he concludes with a joyful July 4 comment: "We have celebrated this memorable day. . . . The camp resounds with 'hurrah for the 4th.'"[3]

Echols's expedition arrived in Fort Davis on July 10 and left on the fourteenth after replenishing their supplies—including new shoes for the men. The expedition marched along the west side of the Chisos Mountains toward Presidio on the Rio Grande, probably following the springs and surface water in the Alamito watershed.

Echols reached the Comanche Trail leading to San Carlos, Mexico, and wrote that they had marched down an arroyo he called "Lates Lengua" [Terlingua Creek] (Fig. 3.1). On July 25, he noted: "We went to the river this morning . . . to see a wonderful curiosity . . . a place where a stream runs through a mountain precipice about 1500 feet high. The opening is just the width of the stream . . . the precipice springing vertically from the water to its summit."[4]

As you photograph Santa Elena you might be standing where Lieutenant Echols and the camels stood as they viewed the canyon for the first time. Imagine the exhausted group as they reached the water flowing from the canyon he called "Gran Puerta" [Great Door]. As they stood at the canyon portal, those camels, mules, and men were surely the strangest assortment of "tourists" ever to visit Santa Elena Canyon.

It was the Pecos River, however, that presented ongoing challenges to everyone. The Pecos River's claim to fame was its disagreeable nature. It had been the nemesis of travelers east and west since recorded history began. For sixty miles, before its confluence with the Rio Grande, the Pecos flows through a deep canyon, and, of necessity, all the early trails angled north for fifty miles to the flatland crossings at Fort Lancaster and beyond. Even there, crossing the Pecos was a dangerous chore for the conquistadors, as well as the pioneers, military troops, and early cattlemen. Many stories are told about their difficulties with the smelly, muddy river bottoms and steep, unstable banks. The early Spaniards dubbed it the Río Salado [Salt River] and the Río Puerco [Piglike or Dirty River].

It was 1923 before the Highway Department carved a narrow road into each side of the canyon and bridged the river. This shortened, by one hundred miles, the trip from Del Rio to Langtry. When the road was completed, everyone along Highway 90 celebrated their good fortune in finally having the "finest, shortest and best road from coast to coast." It was a Very Important Bridge.

3.1. Terlingua Creek, or Lates Lengua, as Lt. W. H. Echols dubbed it, is surrounded by bluffs and projecting ridges. Colors and contrasts are subtle but beautiful. Late afternoon is the best to view the bluffs of Lates Lengua.

3.2. The pharmacy in this photo is typical of the structures at Fort Davis before renovation.

In 1954, the Pecos went on a rampage. Record-breaking rains caused an avalanche of floodwater and brought down the steel bridge. It was reportedly the second heaviest rainfall ever recorded in the world, and it brought death and destruction to the Pecos and Rio Grande valleys. The Highway Department replaced the steel bridge with a temporary low-water concrete slab. The slab washed away the following year and was quickly replaced with a second slab just in time to permit the dedication ceremony of the beautiful "new" bridge you cross today.

"The First Day of Crossing" in the spring of 1957 was held to celebrate the completion of this marvelous high bridge. Today it still stands strong—1,310 feet long and 280 feet high—above a narrow finger of water that is part of Amistad Dam on the Rio Grande upriver from Del Rio.

The depth of the canyon is easy to miss, since most drivers are more concerned with staying on the bridge, and in the right-hand lane. However, I hope you will stop at the roadside park east of the crossing and take a long look at this historic canyon. If you look closely you will be able to locate the roadbed down to the original bridge and the low-water crossing.

Fort Davis is the county seat of Jeff Davis County. The name was chosen to honor secretary of war Jefferson Davis.

The post at Fort Davis had been manned for only six years when the Civil War began and the Union troops were ordered to withdraw. For a time, the 2nd Texas Mounted Rifles occupied the buildings. After their departure, Indians reclaimed their land and renewed their raids upon the travelers and the few settlers who remained in the area.

The crude buildings deteriorated and were barely livable when Lt. Col. Wesley Merritt arrived in 1867 and began construction on a new fort with sturdy buildings of limestone and adobe (Fig. 3.2). These are the buildings that were restored in 1963 by the National Park Service and are the ones you see today. The fort has been called the finest existing example of a frontier post in the nation.

3.3. A color guard composed of members of the 10th Cavalry Association who acted in the historical documentary filmed at Fort Davis a number of years ago are shown here. The association is composed of a full company of men with authentic cavalry equipment and uniforms belonging to the original soldiers during the most active period at Fort Davis, 1865–1890.

For the next fifteen years, the black soldiers of the 9th and 10th Cavalry and the 24th and 25th Infantry were assigned here to guard and patrol the Texas frontier. Many of these men were former slaves recruited from the South after the Civil War and were called Buffalo Soldiers by the Indians because of their curly hair. They were brave soldiers who earned a proud record for fearless service. They were involved in important campaigns to ensure the safety of the settlers, the freighters, mail, and stagecoach travelers (Fig. 3.3).

During the time Col. Benjamin Grierson commanded Fort Davis, he established several outlying posts at major water holes throughout the Big Bend Country. One of these outposts was at Neville Springs.

Neville Springs is one place near upper Tornillo Creek that could have been called an oasis. There was an abundance of free-flowing water there providing for the needs of the military and their livestock. One day I turned over a flat rock next to the ruins and found it marked with initials and date—"WAK 1896."

Fort Davis was abandoned in 1891, when the last Apache chief, Geronimo, surrendered and Indian problems finally came to an end, but it is possible that a detail remained to keep an eye on the Comanche Trail only a few miles away.

The National Park Service is now charged with the responsibility of conserving the historic documents and heritage of Fort Davis. Special programs often include military parades with color guard and music. Interpretive staff members dressed in military uniforms of the 1880's explain activities, events, and the daily routines of the men at the fort. The men pictured in my photographs were members of the 10th Cavalry Association who appeared in a documentary film made at Fort Davis in 1977. They are carrying authentic cavalry equipment and wearing uniforms like those worn by the 10th after the Civil War.

My friend Barry Scobee, who lived most of his life in the town of Fort Davis, was one of the most knowledgeable folks in West Texas. He wrote reams of copy, scores of articles, and several books on West Texas history. His files included cartons bursting at the seams with a wealth of historical material (Fig. 3.4). His books were dog-eared and worn from many readings.[5]

I'm sure some of his material dated back to the time between 1871 and 1885, when Fort Davis was the county seat of the original Presidio County. [In 1887, Presidio County was divided into three counties: Jeff

3.4. Surrounded by his books and a few of his files, Barry Scobee shows one of his albums containing clippings and photos. Periodicals and books overflowed shelves and grocery cartons. Scobee's was a valuable collection of material on early Fort Davis.

3.5. Today, Fort Davis is host to the thousands of visitors coming to see Fort Davis National Historic Site, which is being restored to much of its former glory. In pioneer days, the Overland Trail served the first wave of travelers and wagon trains heading west.

Davis, Brewster, and Presidio—Ed.] Barry interviewed those who were present at the time "things happened," and their stories enrich the history of Fort Davis.

Scobee came to Fort Davis from San Antonio in 1917 and assisted Carl Raht in gathering material for his book *The Romance of Davis Mountains and Big Bend Country* first published about 1918. Scobee wrote in detail about skirmishes between the Buffalo Soldiers and the Apaches, and of pioneer travelers along the Overland Trail, which passed just beyond his office window.

In 1964, Barry Scobee was honored by having a mountain just east of Fort Davis named in his honor. The dedication program of Barry Scobee Mountain was led by Texas governor John Connally.

You would have enjoyed traveling the seventy-six-mile Davis Mountains Scenic Loop with Barry, as I did in 1976. He would have suggested that you pack a picnic lunch, as several roadside parks are located along the way in historic and interesting shaded areas. For centuries the Indians used many of these same sites for their hunting camps.

Begin your trip by driving west of Fort Davis on Highway 17, which is also the historic Overland Trail—the road across the plains to the newly discovered goldfields in California (Fig. 3.5). The trail was renamed the Butterfield Road after the official Overland Trail shifted its route farther north. At other times in its history, Barry said it was variously known as El Paso Road, the San Antonio–San Diego Road, the Lower Road, the Jackass Mail Route, and other colorful names I will not mention here.

You might want to photograph the picturesque county courthouse as you pass. Justice of the Peace Barry Scobee had his office there.

Turn right when you get to State Highway 166 at the eastern edge of town. Nearby you will see the historical marker dedicated to the memory of Henry Skillman, a stagecoach entrepreneur of the Overland Trail. Skillman had a contract to see the mail safely through the Big Bend Country three times each week. He also made use of his other talents as guide and Indian scout for both federal and Confederate troops and had a reputation as a "feisty desperado."

In 1890, the Rev. W. B. Bloys held religious services for forty-eight people while standing on an Arbuckle Coffee crate at the Skillman Grove campground. Townsfolk and ranch families gathered each year in mid-August for this annual Cowboy Camp Meeting. They slept in their wagons or tents. Meals were prepared and shared by everyone. Today, this ecumenical camp meeting is still an annual summer event which draws thousands to the site.

Scobee pointed out the gap near Sawtooth Mountain used by ranchers to trail thousands of cattle northward to the Panhandle and markets beyond, until the Southern Pacific railroad tracks were laid across the state in 1882 and spelled the end of the long cattle drives. Some of those original pioneer ranch families still have descendants living in the area.

After you leave the gap at Sawtooth Mountain where the mountain slopes extend toward the plains, massive boulders can be seen. See if you can locate places on the rocks where Indians rubbed fat from deer and buffalo hides on the rough boulders. Rubbing of the hides gave the rocks a smooth polish. At "Rockpile," a roadside picnic area, Scobee showed me the rock where Kit Carson had taken time to carve his name. The inscription is dated "Dec 25, 1839."

As you ascend the slopes of Mount Locke, you are also traveling the highest public road in Texas. It reaches an elevation of 6,791 feet. The clear, salubrious mountain atmosphere created an appropriate location for McDonald Observatory. It was built in 1926 by the University of Texas. The first telescope was dedicated in 1939 and became the second-largest telescope in the world. It made the Davis Mountains facility one of the great observatory complexes. The observatory continues to expand in size and prominence. Public viewing is scheduled but tour reservations are required. You might also enjoy attending one of the evening outdoor "star parties" led by a knowledgeable member of the staff. You will have an opportunity to view the planets, moon, and/or stars through large telescopes and ask questions of the tour leaders. Take binoculars—and don't forget your coat!

The National Radio Astronomy Observatory is only a few miles away on the valley floor. These two facilities bring many of the world's finest scientists to Fort Davis.

As you leave McDonald Observatory, your leisurely drive will continue down Limpia Canyon to Keesey Canyon and the twenty-seven hundred–acre Davis Mountains State Park. It is the site of picturesque Indian Lodge. I recommend to visitors this pueblo-style building as an overnight stop. There are a campground, RV park, and picturesque dining room in the park also. The state park lodge was among the first projects built in Texas by the Civilian Conservation Corps in the 1930's. One of my favorite rest areas is at the top of the hill south of Indian Lodge. The view of Fort Davis below will help you visualize its interesting history.

After homemade pie and coffee at Indian Lodge, Barry and I returned to Highway 118 and continued south along Limpia Creek. Limpia Creek is lined for much of its course by groves of cottonwoods and other deciduous trees. In autumn, rich golden colors reflect in crystal-clear pools. Towering above the trees and creek are miles of ruggedly beautiful red-rock palisades. No matter what time of day or quality of light, this is country worth photographing and sharing with others.

On your left you will pass a shady cottonwood grove beside Limpia Creek where Scobee said Antonio de Espejo camped with his entourage in 1582–1583. Espejo came north from Mexico along the Río Conchos and was headed for the Pecos River, which he intended to follow farther north to Santa Fe, New Mexico. His entourage included his scribe, Luxán, fifteen soldiers, and a hundred horses and mules.

Espejo was a rich fugitive from Spanish law. His Franciscan friend, Fray Beltrán, convinced him that an important discovery of gold or silver in this unknown land might result in dismissal of the charges against him. Because of Luxán's clear references and description of their camp along Limpia Creek, we can say that Espejo's group became the first recorded Europeans to enter the Davis Mountains. Scobee believes their camp was just north of the fort's pump house and well.[6]

When you reach the junction of Highway 17, a left turn will have you back on the historic Overland Trail traveling east toward Wild Rose Pass. A right turn will bring you back for further exploration of the historic and delightful town of Fort Davis.[7]

Smuggling and Other Career Paths

Amor Eterno

An unknown love
Of one hundred years,
Side by side they lay
In Lajitas stone
Quenched by the Big Bend Sun
Their love was renewed
As their Christian crosses
Touched each other
As if holding hands
In God's Paradise of Eternal Love

B. J. Gallego

THERE WERE THREE OF US in the old black Ford when we started out just after dark. Creaking and groaning, the truck slowly bumped its way over an unimproved road to a well-known Rio Grande crossing in the lower Big Bend Country. The moon was rising over the scrubby mesquite and willow trees when we reached a small clearing on the riverbank. The tailgate was quietly lowered and a platform scale put in place, ready for business. We waited silently in the shadows of the river cane.

A rendezvous had been arranged to meet a burro train loaded with candelilla wax, and I had been invited to watch the operation. My worries eased a bit when I learned it was not illegal in the United States to receive the wax, although it violated Mexican law. [At the time, Mexico had established quotas and had placed a limited embargo on shipments out of the country.—Ed.]

Candelilla is a plant found growing in the lower desert hills on both sides of the Rio Grande. It can be identified by its clusters of bare, 18", slim-as-a-pencil stalks of a greenish gray color. The candelilla plants are harvested by hand, root and all, and brought by the burroload to wax camps, where the wax is rendered by placing it into vats of boiling water. A little sulfuric acid is added so the paraffinlike wax will float to the surface. After it cools, the crude wax is skimmed from the top and sent to market for further refinement and distribution. It is used both as a hardener and a solvent in products as varied as saddle soap, cosmetics, paint remover, and chewing gum.

Soon a rustling in the river cane and muffled voices announce the arrival of the pack train. Friendly greetings are exchanged and a brief business consultation is followed by whispered jokes about the quality of the wax, the amount of dirt and gravel, and accusations regarding the accuracy of the scales. When the weighing begins, sacks of crude wax are transferred hastily from the burros to the scales then loaded onto the truck. I watch as everyone works to speed up the exchange.

One of the Mexican workers on the truck occasionally hoists a sack of wax back down to an amigo waiting to receive it. That fellow takes it behind the burros, back to the scale—to be weighed again. No one seems to notice. The buyer at the scale adjusts the balance bar to show less weight. More sacks are hoisted, more fumbling with the balance bar. When the weighing is finished, a bottle is passed around. Money changes hands. Then burros, smugglers, and *dinero* disappear back into the river cane.

Each side believes it came out ahead, but my guess is that things were about even.

A different kind of smuggling took place along the deserted border crossings in Pancho Villa's days. The most popular item at that time was an assortment of arms and ammunition. One old-timer, who claimed to be a "pretty good smuggler," was in a reminiscent mood when he told me about "the good old days," when he successfully defended his trail against outsiders' use.

"I tell you what! You can't let everyone use your trail if you have a good one. Attracts too much attention. Brings in the law," he said.

A portion of his trail followed a narrow shelf near the edge of a cliff for several hundred yards. Anyone on the trail would be silhouetted against the sky—an easy mark for him, as he and his rifle lay concealed among boulders at the base of the cliff:

> I usually killed their leading pack burro first. If they didn't stop and turn back when it tumbled off the cliff, I shot at the first man. That usually stopped the parade. If not, they were boxed in by my helpers at both ends. As they turned back I dropped a couple more burros. What the animals carried we took for our trouble. I always made an honest split with my helpers.
>
> Sure, I made enemies. Never did show myself until I saw who was closing in on my house. If I walked out to talk, my wife was aiming a rifle on him from the window. Fact is, she'd rather kill a man than me.

Many visitors ask how families make an "honest" living along the Rio Grande. Candelilla wax supported a few families some years ago, but far more residents on both sides of the river have always been successful at ranching, farming, trapping, and hunting. Between 1900 and 1942, hundreds were employed in the quicksilver mines.

4.1. The store, a few cabins, a church, and a school were all abandoned when the mines closed in 1942. Only a few people remained in the Terlingua ghost town when this photo was taken.

4.2. The Perry house dominates the landscape at Terlingua, and all who were employed at the Chisos mines constantly felt the impact of this tough New Englander either by his presence or a view of his pretentious house from their doors and windows.

The Chisos mine was located at the current "ghost town" of Terlingua and had the longest period of operation and the greatest production of any mine in the area. Today, it is hard to imagine Terlingua as home to over twelve hundred residents. Among them were the Mexican Americans who deserted their village, Terlingua Abaja, and moved ten miles north to work in the mine at Terlingua. They built jacals and new flagstone-adobe huts, as time allowed, on the flat below mine owner Howard Perry's desert "mansion" (Figs. 4.1 and 4.2).

Meanwhile, the old village of Terlingua Abaja, three miles up Terlingua Creek from Santa Elena Canyon, became a melted-adobe ghost town. Macario Hinojos told me some of the houses at Terlingua Abaja were ancient ruins when his people were living there a hundred years ago.

The area now appeals only to bird-watchers or photographers who want to find one more scene of historic ruins, eroded desert flats, and distant, wrinkled mountains.

The Terlingua area mines produced mercury, also called quicksilver, which was processed from the red cinnabar ore abundant at several locations in the area. It was in high demand during the early 1900's. The southern Brewster County mining district produced more than 150,000 flasks of mercury weighing seventy-six pounds each. [Primary uses of mercury at that time included thermometers, detonators, and blasting caps.—Ed.] The flask value varied with market conditions, but the Chisos mine probably produced over three million dollars worth of liquid mercury between 1903 and 1942, when it closed.

Mine owner Howard E. Perry was a tough, rich New Englander. He was a mysterious power, unknown except to a few close associates, and none of them ever talked much for the record. No one ever complimented him, and he had equally low regard for his employees. He had a reputation as a sly and devious competitor. The Chisos mine was accused more than once of tunneling into competitors' mining properties.

Mexican American employees gave him the nickname of "*pantalones*," because he always wore knickers when he visited the mine. But most called him "Chapo" or "Chapo Pérez."

The first, and very primitive, hundred-mile road from the mines to the railroad terminal in Marfa cost well over $100,000 to build. The round-trip took freighters from ten days to two weeks, depending on the weather. Wagon trains usually consisted of three to ten heavy Studebaker wagons, each pulled by eight to twelve mules. Each wagon was loaded with three to four tons of ore. On the return trip, the wagons were loaded with food and supplies for the mining camps. [The wagons were used as late as the mid-1930's.—Ed.]

The end of Perry's empire was noted by the sheriff of Brewster County in a legal notice in the *Alpine Avalanche* on August 19, 1942: "On October 6, 1942 . . . at the Court House Door of Brewster County, Texas, I will offer for sale and sell at public auction, for cash . . . the property of the Chisos Mining Company."

But even before this legal pronouncement, much of the small equipment had been carried off—legally or otherwise. It seems to be the custom along the border for all who remain to help themselves to whatever is left by those who depart.

Many people chose to move on when the Terlingua area mines closed in 1942, and the population dropped from twelve hundred to twenty-five inhabitants. By 1950, a river rider and an elderly woman were the only two residents (Fig. 4.3).

Earning a living during the 1940's became a creative endeavor. Lower Brewster County's new hope for a prosperous future remained dim for several years, until the development of Big Bend National Park brought increased tourist traffic and trade to the area.

4.3. *The Terlingua cemetery is a visitor attraction during most of the year. When the mines closed, many of the graves were decorated with wreaths, handmade from baling wire. Gaily painted flowers were painstakingly cut from cans and hung on the wooden crosses. Now, after time and vandals have done their work, it is a sad place, in contrast to the Chili Cookoff, which takes place nearby.*

In the meantime, those with ingenuity found a way to accumulate enough cash to purchase life's essentials. Most small desert communities had a trading post, cantina, post office, teacher, and barber. Some used their burros or wagons to haul wood and water for the remaining residents for a fee. Some were skilled at making adobe brick or rock masonry. Ruben Ortiz made his living collecting cactus.

I met Ruben one day in 1975 as I walked back to the car after a day of photography near Lajitas. He too was headed home after a day's work. The panniers on two of his burros were full of cactus. The burro he was riding had its head up, ears pointed forward, and the bell around its neck clanged in an offbeat syncopation with the muffled clattering of unshod hoofs on the pavement.

The species of cactus that Ruben collected for more than eighteen years were sold in small display cartons you may have seen for sale along our highways years ago.

I had always believed that commercial collecting had cleaned out most of the desirable desert plants; however, watching Ruben work I saw that this was not true. He collected plants of a certain salable size and allowed all others, the large, the small, and the malformed, to remain. I would estimate that only one in five was taken. Those remaining would produce seed to perpetuate the species. This proved to me it was not the collecting Ruben did that cleaned out many of the desert plant varieties. That transgression falls upon outsiders with no respect for the desert. For that reason, it is now illegal to collect any cactus at all.

Bill and Jimmie Cooper knew just about everyone in the Big Bend, since they ran the store and gas station at Persimmon Gap during the early 1940's. The couple met when Jimmie was hired to teach at the Persimmon Gap one-room school on the Cooper family ranch. Later, they lived at San Vicente, where Jimmie taught school in the 1930's. She wrote this description of Margarita de la Rosa, a colorful customer from Mexico who occasionally visited Bill and Jimmie at their small San Vicente trading post:

> Many called him "old leather britches." He wore "gamusa" (immaculately tanned deer-hide clothes) [chamois—Ed.], which he made. He was a tall, copper-skinned individual, blue-eyed, and with a white beard and hair. In spite of his age he sat his horse as erectly as he walked.
>
> His piercing eyes were accustomed to great distances, and were keenly alert. . . . His long tapering fingers were educated to the skill of throwing as well as making a fine maguey rope. He lived in the Fronteriza Mountains south of the border.
>
> A real vaquero—this leather britches—and he rode the best horse I had ever seen cross the river. . . . He told me he owned a large ranch, had many boys, and a wife who operated his ranch while he attended a traveling school, in Chihuahua, Coahuila and Saltillo Mexico.[1]

The school sessions were taught by circuit-riding "men of religion," and Jimmie said each session lasted about three months.

Polk Hinson's place in Study Butte was a delight to early Big Bend National Park employees and area ranch families. Study Butte was named for early-day prospector and miner Will Study [rhymes with "duty"]. Polk's Place was a good place to hear the latest news, have a cold beer, and buy a few groceries. If the generator was turned on you could even dance away the evening. Polk kept his archaic jukebox running by treating its innards gently with the pliers he kept handy in his hip pocket—and by never changing the big 78 rpm records.

Early-day Big Bend photographer W. D. Smithers once told me about one of the old-timers who spent a lot of time trapping beaver along the Rio Grande. The trapper's name was James McMahon. Back in 1899 he accompanied Maj. Robert T. Hill on his exploratory trip through the Big Bend canyons. Since he'd been trapping the area for years, James McMahon may have been the first Anglo to explore the Big Bend canyons.

According to Smithers, it was about 1921 when he came upon James, then in his seventies, camped near Boquillas on a trapping trip from El Paso to Del Rio.

McMahon invited Smithers to join him at his campfire and share his feast. Smithers accepted his offer. Out of the coals and ashes the trapper brought a polecat which he'd skinned, cleaned, and baked for hours in a thick casing of river mud. With less-than-enthusiastic interest, Smithers ate a bit of the skunk, and although he admitted it tasted pretty good, he suddenly discovered he no longer had an appetite and excused himself from a second helping.

Another colorful trapper who lived in the Big Bend in the early days was Henry "Bobcat" Carter. Carter was known to tell folks that, during his lifetime as a trapper, he'd "pizened everything from sugar ants to elephants." The last years of his life he lived at Persimmon Gap in a tin barn on Bill Cooper's property.

Bill said when he was a boy Carter told him, "Never throw away a shirt when the buttons [pop] off, as many wasteful people do. Instead, just put another shirt on over the old one. That helps to keep the cold out. When the toe of a sock wears out . . . just shove your foot through the sock and pull it up on your leg." To show what he meant, he hoisted a pants leg and revealed to young Cooper about ten or twelve old socks on his shanks.[2]

"Another way to keep your feet warm," Carter once confided to Bill with a wink, "is to put a little pepper in your shoes!"

Boquillas, Mexico, was settled in 1896, when lead and silver deposits were discovered in Mexico's Sierra del Carmen. The mine, called Minas

Ricas, was about five miles into the mountains by trail. From Boquillas a cable tramway was built to carry the ore across the river so it could be transported by truck to the Southern Pacific railroad at Marathon for shipping. In later years, fluorspar [a mineral used as a flux in smelting operations—Ed.] was also mined and transported to the rail siding at Marathon. [Incidentally, Boquillas is another area where men are still harvesting the candelilla plants. The yellowish wax is now legally sent south to Cuatro Ciénegas, Coahuila, for processing and sale.—Ed.]

For many years, Boquillas's main tourist attraction was a burro ride across the Rio Grande to visit the picturesque Cantina Padilla and enjoy a "cool one" at the bar. The bar was hand-carved by Dionisio Padilla in 1884 at Cuatro Ciénegas, Coahuila, and brought 150 miles by wagon to Boquillas. It has heard countless secrets and served many a thirsty rancher, smuggler, and outlaw in its lifetime.[3]

H. A. Ernst was justice of the peace at La Noria. He was also the all-powerful ruler of an "empire" stretching a hundred miles along the Rio Grande and for about seventy-five miles toward Marathon. This put Ernst in control of all the water holes between Boquillas and Double Mills.

A second settlement along the old road was at McKinney Spring, where a grocery and, in all probability, a cantina served the freighters, locals, and "transients." Since the Rio Grande and Mexico were less than a day away on horseback, "men of ill repute" were plentiful. [According to an "Old West" tradition, no one ever asked a stranger who he was, where he was from, or what his business might be.—Ed.]

Ernst thought he had a good thing going at La Noria, or Ernstville, as he called it. Mules pulled the heavy ore wagons up the long grade from Boquillas, and the sweating animals arrived in La Noria greatly in need of water. Apparently, Ernst took advantage of the freighters and their mules by selling them a "token to water one animal."

Knowledge of the water tokens was discovered when some folks from Hobbs, New Mexico, found one of the round disks, about the size of a quarter, near the Pecos River north of Fort Stockton, according to a report in the *San Antonio Express*.

At La Noria, flat places were cleared near Ernst Tank, or Tinaja, for wagons to pull off the road. Men could water their teams, replace broken gear, and settle the dust in dry throats. It was another day's journey to the next water hole. No need for a token there—only a prayer for the wagon and team to hold up for the rest of the journey into Marathon.

Justice of the Peace H. A. Ernst was ambushed, shot in the back,

and killed in September of 1908, a short distance from the present-day
location of the park tunnel near Boquillas, by unknown "outlaws" who
satisfied their difference of opinion with the King of Ernstville.

In 1899, the Lajitas Trading Post was established by H. W. McGuirk.
He donated some of his land for a mission and a school. In 1904, he was
licensed to operate a post office. In 1915, the Lajitas Trading Post was
run by Thomas V. Scaggs.[4]

In 1941, the trading post was purchased by Rex Ivey and in recent
years his son Bill has served the international trade. The river crossing at
Lajitas has had a "variegated" history, since it is located at a major crossing of the Comanche-Apache War Trail. In earlier times, the crossing
saw not only explorers and traders but a motley assortment of bandits
and thieves.

During the Mexican Revolution, an island in the middle of the river
was neutral ground upon which Texas ranchers and Mexican cattlemen
met to negotiate the price of unbranded Mexican livestock. "Some of
the strangest and largest cattle trades in history took place on that
island, with Texas traders squatted on bootheels opposite mustachioed
Mexican revolutionists or bandits, a handkerchief spread between them,
its corners weighted with rocks. Thousands of head of cattle waited on
the island while the traders stacked gold coins on the handkerchief and
drove the best bargains they could. The Mexicans were fighting for a
[revolutionary] cause [in 1917] and were desperate for money. The Texans had the money; their position was protected by guns; and no one
doubts that they drove shrewd bargains."[5]

The Lajitas cemetery is a poor man's cemetery, as are most of those
found in the small border villages. On occasion, I visit the cemetery to
pay my respects at the grave of Macario Hinojos. I first met Mac when
he worked in Big Bend National Park during the 1940's, as did other
men from the river villages. Mac was loading a string of Park Service
burros with lumber when we met. That summer he made daily trips
from the Basin to Boot Spring with materials to build the cabin which
would house the seasonal fireguard.

The graves in the Lajitas cemetery are mostly simple mounds covered with a layer of heavy rocks. Here and there a wooden cross is held
in place—almost—with blocks of heavy limestone. At Mac's grave I saw

4.4. *Patti (left), Betsy, and June visit Luna's jacal shortly after the family moved away. Luna's home was partly cave, but the entrance was the old jacal tradition of sticks, adobe, and stone. The roof could be covered with cane fronds in the summer to keep the interior cooler.*

weathered wreaths of paper flowers, cobbles of agate and colorful rock decorating his grave and those of other members of his family. These graves are rough and rugged symbols of their home and life on earth.

I searched carefully for a camera location where I could catch the spirit, hope, and respect that must be expressed by those who survive. The roughly fashioned crosses symbolize hope, and the towering mountain, Lajitas Mesa, is a worthy monument to the lasting spirit of Mac and all the enduring people of the Big Bend frontier.

Imagine your home nestled among colorful cliffs and boulders with a broad view of the surrounding desert that includes a sweeping vista of Sierra Ponce, Santa Elena Canyon, and Mesa de Anguila. If you'd like to visit such a home, come with me to Gilberto Luna's place (Figs. 4.4 and 4.5).

After crossing the much-divided Alamo Creek on the gravel road twelve miles south of Maverick Junction, we will find Luna's jacal. "His 'jacal' is a cave-like structure made out of ocotillo wood and mortared rocks, with cottonwood limbs between rafters for the roof." This is how it was described by Demencio C. Luna Jr. of Alpine, whose father was born in the jacal in 1920: "In a way . . . you could say that my grandfather and his family were modern day cavemen. They lived a very primitive life style, but they were very happy. My grandfather [Gilberto] was born around 1840 in Durango, Mexico where he lived for many years . . . In 1901, at the age of sixty he crossed the Rio Grande into the United States. . . . [to live and work] at Lajitas as well as Terlingua. . . . He produced and reared a total of fifty-eight children and stepchildren. The greater number of his children lived all of their lives in Mexico."[6]

Demencio Luna said his father lived in his Alamo Creek jacal for twenty-five years. He raised a few goats and farmed the area across the road. He hauled water for his family and his crops in his mule-drawn wagon from a spring several miles away. The water was collected in an

4.5. Although Luna's life was primitive, he lived in his jacal for twenty-five years and left behind a unique memorial to frontier life.

old oil drum and measured out with an ancient gourd dipper to each plant individually. Corn was planted in depressions. Melons were widely spaced and planted with squash near Alamo Creek, where their stout roots would reach subsurface moisture soaking the ground during runoffs. Beans were planted in rows but tightly massed to make use of the dense shade the leaves cast in reducing the earth's temperature.

No matter how hard the times, Gilberto was always the same stoic individual. If he was hungry, he did not show it. If crops were wiped out by a deluge of rain or hail, he salvaged what he could or replanted if he had the seed.

When Luna and his sons farmed the flat beside Alamo Creek, the creek bed was four or five feet higher than it is now. But it is still remarkable to me that Luna, with his oil drums and dipper, could keep his crops alive.

Gilberto Luna was 108 when he died in Alpine, Texas, in 1947.

Many people are amazed at the rugged lives led by the Luna family and other residents along the Rio Grande. I believe these self-sufficient people of the border symbolize the survivors—if civilization, in the name of peace, destroys itself.

LONGHORNS AND PRONGHORNS

Texans might brag that the Big Bend dust is the world's finest—and it is—but keep it out of your camera.

Peter Koch

J. FRANK DOBIE, in *The Longhorns*, describes longhorn cattle as "tall, bony, coarse-headed, thin-flanked, some of them grotesquely narrow-hipped, some with bodies so long that their backs swayed, big ears carved into outlandish designs, dewlaps hanging and swinging in rhythm with their energetic steps, their motley colored sides as bold with brands as a relief map of the Grand Canyon—mightily antlered, wild eyed, this herd of full grown Texas steers might appear to a stranger seeing them for the first time as a parody of their kind."[1]

However, grotesque or not, it was the rangy longhorns left behind by Coronado and other Spanish explorers four to five hundred years ago which might claim the title of "first European settlers."

They adapted so well to the country that by the 1880's there were millions of them wandering the western prairies along with herds of wild horses also left behind by the conquistadors. The cattle, sleeping by day and foraging at night, were pretty much ignored by the Indians, who preferred to hunt the more placid bison. A great deal has been said about the romanticized life of the cowboy, the cattle trails, and the early ranchers who made the longhorns profitable. But these rangy bovines should also be credited for establishing the State of Texas as "Cow Country." Their value as beef provided the means by which many early Texans emerged from the economic disaster of the Civil War.

Milton Faver was an early freighter and would become one of the first cattle barons to settle in the Big Bend. Faver arrived in Presidio and opened a trading post about 1855. He traded brown sugar, sweet potatoes, and candles to the Indians for their longhorn cattle, moved those cattle up from Mexico, and settled them and his family on Cibolo Creek ranchland in the Chinati Mountain foothills.[2]

The railroad arrived in 1882 and opened the area to settlement. "Men of means" established huge ranches. One of the largest spreads covered 600 sections (384,000 acres) of land. Another that included part of the Chisos Mountains consisted of 180 square miles.

As the years went by, the longhorns were phased out by other breeds of cattle the ranchers introduced to supply the demand for tenderer beef. Although those cantankerous longhorns no longer roam the prairies at will, as they did in Faver's time, there are still remnant herds in the Big Bend today.

Cap (Ira G.) Yates kept a small herd of longhorns on his ranch in the Glass Mountains north of Marathon for many years. Yates allowed them to roam over the rough country of his ranch when they were not confined to a pen of stoutly reinforced eleven-strand fence. In the early 1960's, a team of photographers from Eastman Kodak visited the Big Bend. One of the ranches I took them to was Yates's, where they photographed the longhorns turned out of the corral. Pictures of Cap's longhorns were shown in the Kodak exhibit at New York's World's Fair in 1964–1965. He was mighty proud of his herd.

In the 1970's, you could still see men working the roundup in a manner little changed from the days of the longhorn. I photographed Ted Gray, ranch foreman of the Kokernot 06 Ranch, on his cutting horse working Hereford cattle one day (Fig. 5.1).

Just after sunrise, the first bunch of cattle was herded into the gathering pens by men who had been up since long before dawn. Mother cows with calves were penned in the morning so that branding could begin after lunch. At midday, riders came in to change mounts. The cowboys gathered around the chuck wagon and sat on their heels trading stories, ranch talk, and chuck wagon cooking at its best.

Have you ever had a cup of campfire coffee? Wayne Gard, in *The Chisholm Trail*, describes the strong coffee brewed for the cowboys: "The cook put plenty of Arbuckle's in a pot and boiled it for half an hour. Some called it six-shooter coffee. It was so strong, they said, that it would float a pistol."

Ted Gray claims that

West Texas was a wild place in the late 1930's and early 1940's. Ranchers were anxious to be successful, many were trying to recover from the Great Depression. . . . World events were still in

5.1. The photo shows Ted Gray, former manager of the Kokernot o6 Ranch, and his men. At midday the riders came to camp to change horses and enjoy chuck wagon cooking at its best.

turmoil, and threats of another war appeared daily in the newspaper. Ranchers in south Brewster County stocked their ranches with cattle, sheep and goats, hoping that they could produce and profit from wool, mohair, calves and lambs that could be sold for slaughter. . . .

Ranchers were faced with hard choices and decisions, severe variances in weather conditions, country that was unusually dry, and work that could kill a man. They were business men who worked many hours a day, seven days a week, at rugged physical labor. Given the opportunity to meet with other folks, and celebrate good times, ranchers partied just as hard as they worked.[3]

The Post, about three miles south of Marathon, was the site of a military post in the 1800's. It was built as a Fort Davis outpost to protect the area from warriors on the Comanche War Trail located about ten miles to the east.

A small, attractive lake was formed there by impounding water from the source of Peña Colorado Creek. The Post served as a county park and a place where residents enjoyed a variety of water sports and picnics. It is well known as the site of a public barbecue which attracts thousands of area residents each July 4. Everyone in the country came to enjoy good food and dance to the music of talented musicians. Ted Gray enjoyed the goat-roping contests as well. He once told me, "If you have been to a Marathon goat-roping and the World's Fair there isn't much else in the world worth seeing."

One comment I often heard from visitors when I was manager of the Alpine Chamber of Commerce in the 1960's was, "How do you manage to keep your roadsides so clean?" Of course, the Texas Highway Department is responsible. It spends millions of dollars annually to keep roads clean and safe, but it has help from ranchers who refuse to sell space for billboards. Our citizens appreciate the value of Big Bend's scenic views and prefer the beauty of roadside flowers and mountain vistas to commercial eyesores along our roads and highways.

Did you know that up until the 1940's most of the Big Bend was clear of fences a few miles beyond the communities? About that time, a bunch of prospectors arrived looking for uranium under the blanket protection of a national emergency. They rode roughshod over the country in their Jeeps and caused no end of trouble for the ranchers and their livestock. This was not for the national good, as they claimed, but a greedy search for sudden wealth. It took only a few months for fences to appear, as the ranchers took the necessary measures to protect their property.

The geology of the land south of Marathon is quite interesting. Ages ago, when the sea covered the land, a gigantic ocean trench fourteen thousand feet deep was located at the lower edge of what is now the Marathon Basin. This trench is now filled with the outwash rubble of volcanic action. The floor from the vast depth of an ancient sea was thrust upward to form the Caballos novaculite, or "scalloped hills." They are sometimes related directly to the Appalachian uplift, created by the same earth-forming forces.

Santiago Peak, that symmetrical peak looming on the horizon and seen from the roadside south of Marathon (before you enter the park), is like a massive paperweight that rests on the last evidence of the scalloped upthrust from the east. South of this point the mountains will be igneous intrusives from within the earth, or fractured limestone laid down by the sea.

Sam Nail is a well-known ranch name in the Big Bend Country. Sam ranched about twenty sections above Cottonwood Draw east of Burro Mesa on the Castolon road. The first time I met the rancher it was at the point of his gun. I had crossed his fence, and he wanted to know what I was doing on his land. I explained I was photographing a scene of Oak Creek pour off and the mountains—Carter Peak and Vernon Bailey—which flank it. I wanted the flowering cholla cactus growing in his pasture to be the foreground. Sam lowered his gun and we got acquainted. I like to think we became friends that day.

Sam and his family lived in a modest adobe-frame house from 1918 until the mid-1940's, when Big Bend National Park bought his land.

Some of Sam's ranch ruins remain and are interesting, although melted down to bare adobe. Birds and plants are abundant because the windmill still pumps water into a small pool. Fig and pecan trees planted by the Nails were still growing last time I visited there. The ranch is one of the best sites in the park for bird-watching, and it is easy to reach. There is no closed season on photography, so tear yourself away from your recliner, turn off the television, grab your camera, and sit for a spell under the shade trees at Sam Nail's old ranch.

As you drive the lower part of Ross Maxwell Scenic Drive, you will notice Castolon Peak [Cerro Castellán] to the southeast. It has long been a geological landmark. The layers of colorful strata tower in a single formation above the complex desert land. Millions of years are represented in its composition. In early pioneer days, there was a simple trading post on the American side. South of the Rio Grande a few rock houses and jacals were strung out along the upper riverbank in an old farming community once known as Coyote.

The Castolon Trading Post is now a Big Bend National Park concessions outpost with an interesting history and a snack bar where you can buy something cool and wet to enjoy outside, under the river cane ramada.

When you visit Castolon I hope you can cross the river and visit the ejido village now called Santa Elena.[4] Ejido villages were part of a Mexican federal project which relocated families from worn-out agricultural land to areas where irrigation farming could be practiced. The village of Santa Elena is one of those villages. The town's name comes from Saint Helena, its patron saint.

If you are able to cross the river, your first adventure on this international journey will be crossing the Rio Grande in a flatboat. It takes skillful maneuvering by the crew in a swift current to make a dry landing on the Mexican side. But a visit to the village with its dusty streets, cool cantina, restaurants, school, and church is an experience not easily forgotten. Theirs is a simple life but not without happiness.

On the escarpment towering above the village and farms is a primitive trail which leads toward the village of San Carlos, where the trail crosses a branch of the old Comanche War Trail. It was once the best access route to Mexico's interior from this point on the Rio Grande. Because of the formidable topography of the Sierra Ponce escarpment beyond the village, trails to the south from Castolon and Santa Elena are limited to this one trail. There is another dim, less-traveled route which winds to the left around the base of the mountain. This route has the unique advantage of being available to those "with reason" to bypass settlement.

Texas historian Kenneth Baxter Ragsdale wrote a book about the Johnson ranch called *Wings over the Mexican Border* that details one of the most unusual ranches in the Big Bend.

In 1927, Elmo and Ada Johnson established a ranch and trading post 120 miles south of Alpine, about 16 miles downriver from Castolon. The unstable political situation along the border concerned the U.S. government, and officials asked the Johnsons to allow them to fly reconnaissance flights into the area from Kelly Field in San Antonio to monitor border security. Elmo Johnson used his road grader to clear cactus from a landing strip not far from the ranch house, and, before long, Johnson's ranch became a favored weekend retreat for airmen flying the open-cockpit biplanes of that time.

From San Antonio the pilots followed the Southern Pacific railroad tracks as far west as Dryden, Texas, and then turned southwest for another 120 miles across desert and mountain to the Johnsons', where they were made welcome.

The men enjoyed hunting and fishing, as well as Ada and Elmo's good cooking and hospitality. In 1943, the weekend pleasure trips ended when the airmen went on to World War II overseas assignments. The last signature in the Johnson field register is dated "Nov 25, 1943."

The Civil Air Patrol operated from the airfield for a while, but by April 10, 1944, that had also ended, and a few months later Johnson's Ranch became a part of Big Bend National Park. Today, all that remains of this remote social center are melting adobe walls, drifting dust, and memories.[5]

There is a postscript to this story, however. W. D. Smithers sent the registry book from Johnson's Field to Nathan F. Twining (one of the men who had visited there). At the time, Twining was chairman of the Joint Chiefs of Staff in Washington, DC. In return, Smithers received this letter dated March 1, 1958:[6]

Dear Mr. Smithers:

Thank you very much for sending me the registry book from Johnson's Field. It does bring back some fond memories of the wonderful times we had with the Johnsons during those early days of the Air Force. I will certainly write him a note.

I often think of my first trip down there. Mr. Johnson had a rifle standing in each corner of his house. A young armament officer with us didn't think they were too clean, so he asked Mr. Johnson if he could clean his guns for him. Mr. Johnson said, "Yes, clean all but the one in that corner; that's the one I go hunting with."

I hope some day to go back and see the Big Bend National Park. It must be a very beautiful place.

Thanks again.

Sincerely,
N T Twining

Some years back, when Ray Williams was game warden here, he showed me the best technique for taking photos of pronghorn antelope.

When an antelope herd escapes from danger, he explained, they continue in a line or along one of their trails and will not deviate, even if an eager photographer stands in full view of the herd. This was difficult for me to believe.

He had me take a position near one of their trails. Then he drove his car toward the herd so they would start off in my direction. Sure enough, they kept coming and passed within thirty feet of me. My camera was ready for the picture. It was a good thing because at the speed antelope travel there was no time for camera adjustments or change of focal distance. One blink of the shutter and they'd passed by.

Later I tried it again with a movie camera. The antelope subjects in the movie film were mama and papa and a young one several weeks old. Papa was a real gentleman. He stood in a protective attitude near the camera until the family had moved to safety, then wasted no time joining them. He stood near my blind long enough for me to absorb his sleek beauty. You may have seen antelope in a zoo or animal collection, but a wild creature is so much more vital and alert than a caged one.

The western plains were the habitat of countless thousands of antelope before the ranges were fenced. Since antelope seldom leap fences to forage or escape predators, as deer often do, their number at one time dwindled to fewer than twenty thousand in the western states between Canada and Mexico.

Watch for these beautiful animals while driving the highways east of Marathon to west of Marfa, or across the high country grassland along the Fort Davis, Presidio, or Pinto Canyon roads. Antelope are the swiftest mammals in our hemisphere and have been clocked at sixty miles per hour. They can detect predators from a distance of four miles, so you are not likely to "sneak up" on one. Instead, move your vehicle to the shoulder and slow down to a crawl. Antelope are inquisitive, alert, and aware. If you stop the car, they are long gone. Watch as they race across the country. Their fluid motion seems so effortless—such a delight to watch.

I'm not an avid hunter, but I also had to admire the skill of former Texas Ranger Henry Glasscock. I saw him jump two black-tailed deer from a thicket and shoot them both with a Winchester before they cleared the width of the creek bed. Two bucks. Two shots. Two dead.

I think trophies taken with bow and arrow might be even more meaningful than those taken with a modern game rifle. It certainly takes more skill to hit the mark and requires superior woodcraft for the hunter to approach within range. The hunter must be well acquainted with the territory and familiar with the daily habits of the animals found there. He must know where the animals will go for water, food, and rest. He must also be an expert at stalking.

In these respects, hunting with a bow and arrow is similar to the skills required to photograph antelope, or any other game. Someday I'd like to watch the archers approach their prey and compare their techniques to those of a wildlife photographer.

On my trip in 1948 into the jungles of Suriname [Dutch Guiana], I watched the native Djuka children play hunting games. First they made primitive bows from splints of bamboo strung with gut. They made their arrows of bamboo not much longer than a toothpick. Then, with their eighteen-inch weapon, they shot unfeathered arrows into the eyes of beetles crawling among leaves on the jungle floor. This was their training and practice for the time when they would stand in the bow of a dugout canoe and shoot long, barbed arrows into the eyes of fish lured to the river's surface with bait thrown by the marksman. I have known individuals who developed their skills in hunting or fishing to a high degree, but those children truly amazed me.

My friends Cap Yates, Ted Gray, Henry Glasscock, Bert Beckett, Macario Hinojos, and Polk Hinson were in tune with the country. Some of these men were gifted in the art of conversation and storytelling. Others let their silence speak for their actions, but all of them represented, by example, the true meaning of being at one with the spirit of life in the Big Bend Country.

THE SEARCH FOR
EARLY MAN

*T*his is a plea for the preservation of some tag-ends of
wilderness, as museum pieces, for the edification of those
who may one day wish to see, feel, or study the origins of
their cultural inheritance.

Aldo Leopold

As I LOOK AROUND the Big Bend ecosystem I often try to picture it as it looked eight to twelve thousand years ago. Did the woolly
mammoths, before they became extinct, enjoy a habitat of sparse wood-
lands in the Big Bend? Are the Big Bend paleopeople the ancients who
developed, thousands of years later, the extraordinary Mayan civilization
that existed in Mexico between AD 300 and 900? What other ancient
mysteries await the archeologist's arrival?

I am not a professional archeologist, but it seems to me that
Guadalupe Mountains National Park, 110 miles east of El Paso, could be
an example of how certain areas of the Big Bend might have looked
when paleopeople arrived. In Guadalupe Mountains National Park a live
freshwater stream courses down McKittrick Canyon. A forest of deciduous trees with occasional pines lines the banks and extends up the
canyon wall (Fig. 6.1).

After the Big Bend area began to dry, it might have appeared more
like the area around Capote Creek in southern Presidio County. At
Capote there is an abundance of water at the upper section of the creek,
for the bedrock is below the gravelly soil, which allows moisture to
spread out into areas where tree roots can reach the supply. A fine
growth of ash trees and welcome shade is the pleasant result. At the
lower part of the creek, water flows over bedrock; therefore, little water
is available to the surrounding soil. This, of course, results in smaller
plants.

6.1. One of the most interesting areas in the Big Bend is the Terlingua–Study Butte section. Anyone the least bit inquisitive will find a variety of features of natural and human interest. This view looking across Terlingua Creek toward Tule Mountain may at one time have been similar to the Guadalupe area, in which the paleopeople made their home.

In the Big Bend, I believe the paleopeople had to develop skills far different from those of their distant cousins, the bison hunters of the Plains. They discovered a higher level of culture could be achieved when everyone in the clan shared the hunting, gathering, farming, and processing of food. During the best years, the luxury of leisure time was theirs. They could sit around their campfires, recount tales of courageous exploits and feats of bravery, and develop their language skills.

Rivers and streams offered the paleopeople an easy means of access to the unknown areas of our country and blazed the first trails along many of our watercourses as they crossed from one stream to another searching for desirable hunting grounds. Botanists studying paleolithic times through seed and pollen identification have established West Texas as a far better place than the Plains for man to survive (Fig. 6.2).

The more I explore our dry creek beds, arroyos, and washes, the more convinced I am that scenes such as those at McKittrick and Capote were commonplace in the Big Bend ten thousand years ago.

Apache Canyon is a colorful crimson slash down the western slope of Burro Mesa. The rose-colored flint found in the area is an excellent flaking material. Ancient man worked the cobbles into projectile points and other tools. At many shelters a mound of chips and discarded preforms show the extensive use of Apache Canyon materials. (Preforms are small chunks of rock collected and then sorted to choose those best suited for arrowheads or points. These crude preforms could then be carried to a comfortable area for further work or trade.)

While Apache Canyon chert is found at many locations, other flint types are also abundant. Some were brought in by traders from distant locations and ranged in color from white to gray to red to yellow. Some were spotted like those from the famous Alibates flint quarries in the Texas Panhandle.

Hunting knives, in common use by ancient man, were stoutly fashioned from one piece of basaltic rock. The handheld portion was flaked to fit the hand, and the protruding edge was chipped into a fine point

6.2. Cerro Castellán, also called Castolon Peak, towers above the barren land. It is located a short distance from the historic Castolon Trading Post. Millions of years are represented in its colorful strata, and it has long been a landmark in a unique area.

with sharp edges for cutting. The knife could also be used for gouging, skinning, and dressing game.

Current scientific dating indicates the first hunters arrived in the Big Bend about ten thousand years ago. They found an environment lacking great herds of bison and few places where men could effectively stampede and butcher game forced into death traps by a communal hunt. But they would have had no trouble spearing javelinas. Charging into a herd of javelinas dozing in the cool shade would have sent the animals in all directions in snorting confusion.

A by-product of this hunting concept was the conservation of food resources, although it is doubtful ancient man ever gave it a thought. However, the result is evident. By selective hunting he allowed animals to sustain reproductive levels.

As an example, let us follow two hunters on a typical hunt. Each is armed with a short spear and a handheld basalt weapon like the one described above. Just before daylight they walk silently to an observation point overlooking a stream flowing southward toward the Rio Grande. The men have not hunted this area for some time, but they know that deer, leaving their feeding ground, will soon head toward the stream only a few hundred yards away.

On a distant game trail four does and a buck can be seen moving in their direction. The deer pause with every step to make sure the trail ahead is clear of danger. They finally reach the water and drink—one by one—never crowding. The lone buck stands some distance back and is the last to drink. He then joins the others and leads them to a grove of brush and trees lining the creek bank. One by one they bed down in widely separated places.

Having located the place where the deer will sleep during the heat of the day, the hunters circle upstream, far out of sight, and also rest. They must allow time for the birds and other creatures to accept them without undue alarm.

When the sun is high above them, they decide to make a stealthy approach for a possible kill. They walk into a slight breeze, one man on each side of the creek, and carefully stalk downstream.

A prearranged signal from one hunter to the other warns him a deer has been located. Now only the hunter on the deer's side of the creek moves forward.

Finally, he sees the deer bedded down in the thicket. By watching the ears he can tell when the animal becomes restless. Carefully now . . . ten feet . . . now eight feet separate them.

With a whoop, the hunter leaps toward the opening the deer must use to emerge from the thicket. The deer bounces up—and out. But the hunter is ready. With another whoop, he leaps onto the back of the deer, grabbing an ear and locking his legs under the belly toward the haunches to avoid slashes from the deer's sharp hooves.

His basalt knife is plunged into the throat and rips up and across the neck to cut an artery. He stabs and rips several times as the deer, with its heavy load, struggles up the bank and falls. The other hunter joins his comrade in the final death struggle of their kill.

If this sounds unbelievable, you should know that I have done all except the stab and kill.

My trophy was a fine photograph, as the wild creature looked back, still alive and no doubt confused about what the assault was all about. I learned this capture technique in Ohio from Woody Goodpaster. (I also have vivid recollections of his other lessons, including the capture of live rabbits and pheasants.)

A fine area suitable for a communal deer hunt can be found near the Castolon road. A dry creek bed is at the bottom of the hill before the final grade to Sotol Vista. Look east toward Ward Mountain and you will see numerous volcanic dikes crossing the hillsides. These "rock walls" separate the slopes into numerous browsing areas for deer. A spring on the upper slope provides water, and among the boulders at the base are bedding-down areas (Fig. 6.3).

On the opposite side of the road toward Burro Mesa is a draw which leads to a very narrow canyon. Beyond the canyon is a shelter cave. If this location was used for a communal hunt, a few hunters could slowly herd deer from the upper slopes down through the narrow canyons. Hunters with spears stationed at agreed-upon places could wait for the final drive, which would bring the deer close enough for the kill.

I have visited this Burro Mesa–Ward Mountain site many times and watched deer browsing from one location to another in the narrow canyons, passes, and gaps. The shelter cave below is well located, and bedrock mortars in the creek bed show abundant usage.

It was not until recently, say, a thousand years ago, that the bow and arrow came into popular use. Hunters had to experiment with these new weapons and develop smaller points suitable for deer, antelope, and javelina. The ability to learn new ideas and accept changes such as these is another indication of an advancing civilization. As the people developed new skills, alone or with a companion, and became clever enough to improve their methods, a successful hunter was recognized as an indi-

6.3. Rock shelters and caves were occupied by early Big Bend hunters. Small caves with openings toward the east and south supplemented numerous rock shelters such as this one.

vidual with unusual ability and courage and no doubt assumed leadership of his clan.

When a move to another hunting area became necessary, there were many rocks to provide shelters for people's temporary needs. This freed dependents from the labor of rebuilding primitive shelters. The hunter's clan then had time to experiment with vegetable crops. Even the old and feeble—and the very young—could contribute by trapping or snaring small animals and gathering seeds.

Rock shelters are usually thought of as temporary campsites for transient civilizations. But this is not always the case. The climate in the lower Big Bend Country is such that it requires no more than a windbreak during cold months, openings to catch the slightest breeze during the hot summers, and a limited amount of shade. Huge boulders, so abundant in this area, made it easy to find sites [such as the one in Figure 6.4].

Indian Head is the name of the low mountain north of Rough Run. The huge rocks fallen from the cliffs of Indian Head include small caves

6.4. *Rock shelters and caves occupied by early Big Bend hunters are often located in the vicinity of a prominent landmark. This sheltered cave is an isolated conical hill topped by natural sculpting of the caprock. It has a striking similarity to the temple pyramids of early Mexican civilization.*

with smooth and level floors that would have provided shelter and sites for bedrock mortars. There is evidence this place was occupied by ancient man for thousands of years.

Ever since my first visit to Indian Head to photograph petroglyphs among the boulders, I have felt this place must have been very special to the archaic people who lived there. Anyone sensitive to the environment can feel the tranquillity of isolation and comfortable beauty of the place.

Some of the petroglyphs are similar to those found in New Mexico and Arizona. Their meaning may not be understood today, but they are probably fertility symbols, maps indicating trails, stylized clan signs, and other important symbols. About six boulders, with facets protected from the weather, are decorated with panels of petroglyphs. Their artistic style does not intrude upon the beauty of the scene, nor do they have the impact of a modern bulletin board. A careful study of each panel is a mind-stretching experience, something like listening to a scholarly lecture given in a language not your own. The words, enunciation, voice, and personality combine to present an artistic quality. It can be considered rock art in the truest sense, even without understanding the meaning of the stylized figures, or the graffiti message.

There is a series of small caves lining the base and eroded cliffs above Marty's Run. All of them show signs of being occupied for long periods of time. One has been carefully mapped and searched for material, which I hope will reveal new information in the lifeways of these early inhabitants. Although many sites in the Big Bend have been vandalized, other shelters have collapsed through the ages, thus protecting the important contents beneath for future study.

The first wave of paleomigrants probably settled close to a body of water, which was abundant at that time. One popular place was Grapevine Hills. One of the most extraordinary boulders at Grapevine Hills contains a huge bedrock cistern almost three feet across and over four feet deep. It might hold as much as a metal oil drum. The cistern could have been used as a vat in which persimmons or other fruits were fermented to produce a mild intoxicant. Within a mile of the cistern are many rock shelters which show heavy usage (Figs. 6.5 and 6.6).

Sites dating from the earliest days are often located near a prominent

6.5. Among the maze of boulders at Grapevine are sculptures in the likeness of human forms. Gigantic heads, torsos, and fertility symbols, in addition to this striking scene, are awesome.

6.6. Contrasting types of land are apparent in many parts of the desert. It is hard to imagine the area when much of it was forested.

landmark, perhaps a conical hill topped by caprock sculptures. Perhaps these formations served as landmarks for those returning from the hunt. At the end of the Grapevine Hills Trail is a natural bridge formed by three oddly shaped boulders. The view through this "window" shows details of the valley beyond where an immense collection of sculpted rocks is located. What thoughts do you suppose entered the minds of the people who stood there to survey the land beyond? Do you suppose they were waiting in the early morning light to greet the sun? Or did they give the rocks and scene a deeper meaning? I believe primitive man's mind was influenced to a large extent by this environment and the natural phenomena before which he stood.

When investigating recent sites one occasionally finds unexpected items. In one location I saw bits of bottle glass shaped for use by the Indians. The glass, with its sharp cutting edge, was excellent for cutting tough sinews and muscle or for scraping bone. Near the immigrant route heading west, arrowheads made from barrel hoops and decorative items made from harness buckles, bits, and chains have also been found by archeologists searching more recent sites.

Such finds bring one to the point of expecting anything, but never a handful of beautifully fashioned silver beads. The beads were identified as rosary beads manufactured in Europe about 1720 for Jesuit missionaries. We can speculate on how these religious items wound up at an Indian campsite.

Permanent missions along the border were abandoned during the late 1700's and could have been the place where the beads fell into the hands of marauding Indians. The site where the beads were found is not far from the Comanche War Trail, so it is possible they were carried north from Durango, Mexico. For many years, the Apaches and Comanches raided the *rancherías* to the south each fall and would have carried their loot northward. This answer is probably the best, since lithic works found at the same location were of distinctive Coahuilan-Chihuahuan manufacture.

If you are interested in this subject, begin by reading the history of archaic times or join a historical society and learn about desert research. Then you, too, can actually walk the ancient trails and contemplate their legacy.

As you explore the Big Bend, direct your search toward a closer relationship with the land, its creatures, and all growing things. There is much inherent beauty in the Big Bend that cannot be described. It must be sensed. It is only by physically venturing into the solitude of the desert that the true essence of man's history can reach the depths of your awareness.

Arranging the Snake

by Betsy Koch Clark

I have always been amazed at the patience my father exhibited. He had the artistic need to have everything look exactly the way he wanted it and considered each detail in every picture.

I was eight years old when I met the snake. It was a harmless, gentle snake, a western coachwhip, commonly called a red racer. Dad caught it bare-handed, brought it home in a gunnysack, and hung the bag on a tree limb beside the trailer. The next morning he asked me to help him.

I wasn't eager to get acquainted with the red racer, for I was never a snake lover, but Dad wanted pictures, and before I knew it, I had this snake wrapped around my neck. It felt really yucky!

Dad arranged it precisely after explaining he wanted to take my picture. I rebelled, but he calmed me enough to get through the ordeal. Actually, we went through the "arrangement" several times to find the right pose (the right pose for *me*, as well as for the snake). Then, as always, the sun went behind the clouds and the light wasn't right, so we waited for the clouds to pass. Several minutes went by and it finally came out again. The snake had dropped its head, so Dad went back to rearranging the picture.

The snake must have been tired. He didn't want his head up, so I had to move my hand up closer to his head. Then, another cloud!

Finally, after what seemed like an eternity looking at the snake's tongue sensing the air, I heard the camera click. But once is never enough. Dad always had to have to have several shots in case the light changed or something went wrong in the developing. So he spent more time waiting and arranging while I prayed the whole thing would soon be over.

DESERT DIVERSITY

All archeological material will be of value in future studies *only* if left in place for trained scientists to interpret in relation to its site.

The Back Country

HOT SPRINGS, located at Tornillo Creek's junction with the Rio Grande, is a historic spring used for centuries by archaic Indians. It was developed into a "spa" by J. O. Langford, who homesteaded there in 1909. Langford left in 1942, but Hot Springs remained a busy and well-known landmark in the early days of Big Bend National Park. This was partly due to the engaging personality of Mrs. Maggie Smith, who operated the trading post there for several years.

I, too, enjoyed living at Hot Springs. I operated the trading post for a short time in 1953, after Maggie moved her operation to San Vicente, Texas.

One of my most memorable experiences was a visit with Maggie in early June to see and film the annual rain dance in San Vicente, Mexico. We crossed the Rio Grande in Maggie's truck, because she claimed this dance would bring such torrents of rain the river would rise and an ordinary car would not be able to cross at the ford.

The rain dance ceremony probably arrived in the Big Bend with several pioneer Mexican families who came north from Durango about 1900. They brought their livestock and belongings and settled in the San Vicente area, not far from the abandoned mission built by the Spaniards in 1774.

I have a note that credits José Victorino of San Vicente as the person who may have taught the young men the old customs and traditions and instituted the San Vicente version of the annual rain dance. Descrip-

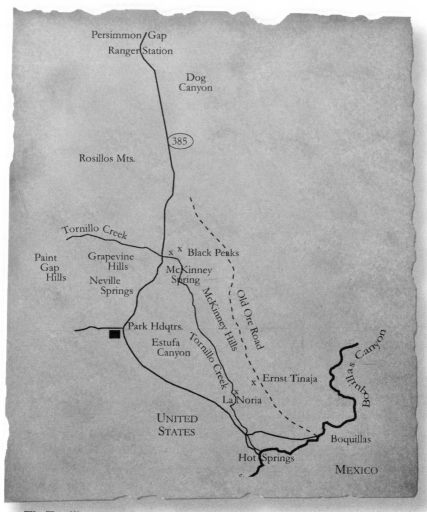

4. The Tornillo watershed

tions of the event vary from place to place and have evolved through the years. The spring ceremony is based on ancient fertility rites, tempered by the priests, to "insure productivity in farm, flock and family" (Figs. 7.1 and 7.2).[1]

The ceremony I attended began just before sunset. The dancers appeared wearing costumes adorned with feathers, tin, and other decorations. They carried special ceremonial bows and arrows in their left hands. A turned-over washtub served as their drum. The tempo of the

7.1. Just a step removed from prehistoric ceremonies is this rain dance enacted at San Vicente as a reminder of ancient beliefs. This ceremony was filmed in 1953.

7.2. The rain dance ceremony may have come to the Big Bend with several pioneer Mexican families from Durango about 1900.

opening was sedate as the entire company of dancers paid respect to a large religious picture. Then the tempo changed to a distinctly archaic, or simple, rhythm and the dance began.

While the opening dance was no doubt mission influenced and the latter part Indian, I found all of it impressive. Finally, they took the cross and the statue of the Virgin Mary, and we went to their presidio. There the dance began again, as the participants once more prayed for God to send them rain. It did not rain that night, as Maggie had predicted it would, but hard summer rains did begin just a few days later.

The next year, Hot Springs was the site of the most spectacular water action I've ever seen in the Big Bend. During a heavy runoff, a rise brought Tornillo Creek's floodwater up to the flat in front of the store. A giant whirlpool circled the base of the cliff and washed away trees on both sides of the creek. The trees circled around and around for hours before they were cast from the whirlpool into the Rio Grande. The San Vicente rain dance that year must have been extraordinary!

If you are staying at the Boquillas campground, you should know about the interesting trail that follows the river upstream to Hot Springs. It was an ancient route long before Langford and Maggie Smith. Now it is highly recommended as a leisurely hike on a deeply worn river trail.

From the Boquillas campground area, the trail contours along the limestone hills toward Hot Springs. Desert vegetation such as lechuguilla, creosote, mesquite, and hechtia lines the trail. A number of large cottonwoods lined the lower Hot Springs area some years ago, but they were girdled and cut down by beaver. River cane and tall weeds remained and now provide a habitat for yellow-breasted chat and wrens. I also suspect that the cane shelters a number of puddle duck species and shore birds during migration. As you near Hot Springs, the trail becomes more distinct as it passes flat-topped boulders at the river's edge, where the bedrock mortars of early Amerinds may be seen.

You might want to stop and soak your feet in the healing waters at the spring. The foundation is all that remains of the primitive bathhouse built by Langford in 1912. The building was partially destroyed in a flood about forty to forty-five years later, but the spring still flows into the shallow foundation that remains and is available to those who wish to enjoy the healing waters.

As you arrive at Hot Springs, where the flagstone cliffs crowd the river trail, watch for a few pictographs. These were drawn before the

river gouged deeper into bedrock, so the simple drawings are now high
above the trail.

Some years ago, the Boquillas–Hot Springs trail was also a river riders'
trail. It was here, along the Rio Grande, that the last line of defense was
formed against the ravages of *fiebre aftosa* from 1946 to 1950. The disease,
called hoof-and-mouth disease on this side of the river, was epidemic in
Mexico, and the governments of Mexico and the United States joined
forces to eradicate the deadly virus affecting cloven-hoofed animals
before it spread to the United States and Guatemala. In rural Mexico
there was mistrust and misunderstanding by the people, who lived far
from newspapers, gossip, and government officials.

The illness of their livestock in the infected areas led to difficult
days. Animals contaminated by the disease were not allowed to wander
across the Rio Grande; to ensure that they didn't, the U.S. government
hired men to ride the river trail. Each river rider was assigned a fifteen-
mile stretch of border trail, which he patrolled twice a day. Any domestic
cloven-hoofed animal suspected of crossing the Rio Grande into the
United States was shot.

Many of the river riders lived in primitive conditions—in a lean-to
or tent close to their section of the river—so all that remains to remind
us of those days are their well-worn trails and the memories they
recorded of a lonesome life along the border. Find the book *The Cow
Killers* in your local library. It was written by Fred Gipson and has
exceptional drawings by Fort Davis resident Bill Leftwich, who participated as a livestock inspector for the Aftosa Commission. Gibson and
Leftwich dedicated the book "to the people of rural Mexico, patient in
the face of men and work they had no way of understanding."[2]

Interesting photo opportunities are presented during the summer
"monsoon season." Shortly after a rain, glistening highlights appear on
creek rocks, adding a color contrast to earth and stone.

I'm often asked what the normal rainfall is in the Big Bend and
Davis Mountains. The answer is anything from ten inches to twice that
much. I don't think there really is a "normal."

Most of the folks who live here would hesitate to quote a firm figure,
but all would agree there are times when the bottom drops out of a black
cloud. Anywhere from three to seven inches can flood the land and
cause a catastrophe instead of a blessing.

The first rain to fall in 1977 in the Study Butte area came in July and started out with a downpour of two inches in twenty minutes.

The flash, crackle, and thunder of lightning was much too close for comfort. Rough Run was a roaring avalanche. Tumbling boulders threatened to demolish the culvert bridge across the highway. Water poured over the bridge, and from the hilltops the scene was one large expanse of fast and angry water. The next morning, only scattered pockets of mud marked the course of the runoff. The dry desert had soaked up the moisture like a blotter.

I once tried to photograph oncoming flood water from the middle of the streambed. The water approached with the growling, rumbling insistence of a freight train. The wall of water was only a foot deep, but the force was so great it caught me unprepared. Rocks and brush carried in the tide tripped me as the leading edge rolled by. My footing, which I thought was secure, was lost as the stream tumbled everything in its path. I fell, holding my camera above the thick floodwater, and with considerable effort crawled sideways toward the bank to escape the turbulent stream. I have never tried *that* clever photo strategy again!

A different sort of experience occurred the day I hiked up a dry creek

7.3. A lizard has been pinned on a thorn by a shrike. The picture was made only minutes after the wiggling creature was captured.

7.4. *I have found it convenient to name some of the locations along Tornillo Creek that I have found interesting. In my file of pictures this one is named Tortilla Flat. I also considered Enchilada Flat before deciding it lacked the necessary color.*

densely crowded with mesquite and catclaw. The desert birds were active. A covey of quail, the young only half grown, flushed from the weeds and announced my arrival. From the center of the thicket a shrike made an uncommon noise, and I quickly climbed a low bank to investigate. I arrived just in time to see the bird impale a lizard on a mesquite thorn, leaving it there for me to photograph (Fig. 7.3). The shrike is a predator whose beak is hooked so it lacks the power to kill. The bird uses thorns like a meat hook to aid in killing and storing food. A lizard will make several meals for the bird. Occasionally, I have seen the shrikes park grasshoppers on a thorn, and in another unusual case, a small bird was impaled, but this was the largest prey I had ever seen taken by this robin-sized bird. The shrike I disturbed waited impatiently nearby to return for his meal.

It is impossible to predict what you, the hiker, might hear or see if you are quiet and alert as you walk in the desert (Fig. 7.4).

Most hikers do not observe changes of temperature when the mid-day heat soars above one hundred. Next time you are in the desert, notice how a slight breeze down a shaded arroyo will feel cool. If a bird flushes from a secluded spot, that may be the place to rest. Additional relief may be found on the shady side of an arroyo. Lie down in the shade, avoiding a place where the sun has been shining all day. If you expect to achieve comfort, there is no substitute for judicious pacing of your every effort. Most hikers are in too much of a hurry. A good rule to remember is, when you perspire, you are going too fast.

Below the Dawson Creek's junction with Terlingua Creek, thin bands of coal are exposed. In the creek bed bits of fossil tree may be found, another proof that this was once a forest of huge trees.

At the present time, the barren land has completed a full cycle from the beaches of an inland sea, lakes, marshes, forest, and, finally, the colorful muds of the Dawson Creek–Terlingua drainage system.

Because of the wide range of color bands from black through the warm color spectrum to off-white, the photographer will find the dome-shaped hills, knifelike ridges, and sparse desert vegetation a challenge to his skill.

Successful photography here demands an early morning or late evening visit. I have found working about three hours after sunrise and three before sunset, spaced out with a siesta or a visit for refreshments at Study Butte, a good schedule. The rounded domelike mounds and contrasting ridges provide opportunities for scenic compositions at a time when long shadows model the scene.

The Painted Desert [now called Maverick Badlands—Ed.] differs from other Big Bend scenics which rely on mountain peaks, erosional remnants of cliffs, caprock, and typical desert vegetation such as yuccas, century plants, and ocotillo. Except for a few scrawny yuccas and nondescript plants, the painted desert relies chiefly on its variety of forms, variety of color, and spacious, open landscape for its effect.

In this lower portion of the Dawson Creek Painted Desert there are a few items which may be considered photographically interesting. Not far from a highline which crosses the area is a fragmented fossil tree. The fragments have the appearance of firewood kindling, even when seen close up. I suppose the only reason it is still in place is that rock hounds know it is soft, limy, gritty, and will not polish.

Meandering through a narrow gap cut by the creek, I found what may be the only metate at a site of an Indian camp. The only reason it remains (you guessed it!) is that the boulder is much too large to carry

7.5. It is a long hike from Devil's Den to K-Bar and much too far when side trips are planned. It is easier to explore along the boulders near K-Bar by parking your car in the parking area near the ranch house and climbing the slope to the rocks.

off. From these two examples, who can say what else might have been located in this land that has had such a variable history.

I had an idea this area would be fine for winter camping (an idea easy to get when summer temperatures pass the hundred mark daily). But I tried it and found it too cold, too windy, with an unmerciful rain that turned to sleet and beat through my clothes until I felt as naked as the slopes around me.

Each time I explore the desert's mysteries, I wish for a more extensive knowledge of geology. Often it takes but a single step to cross from recently deposited sand to that dating to the time of the Inland Sea. At times, the edge of the shoreline is marked by fossilized tree deposits which drifted into pockets where their cell structure was gradually replaced by minerals. Perhaps the prevailing winds of Eocene and Pale-ocene times (fifty-five to sixty-five million years ago) could be deter-

7.6. Mule Ears, located at the southwestern flank of the Chisos Mountains, is a prominent landmark seen from the Castolon Road. On the east side of these peaks, Frank M. Setzler excavated two caves many years ago. In one he found the skeletal remains of three condors. This close-up shot was made using a 105 mm lens.

mined by mapping the location of these fossil tree deposits. The general log drift should be in the direction of the prevailing winds.

On the east bank a short distance above the lower Tornillo bridge is a yellowish bluff. This is said to be an original deposit of silt laid down by the Inland Sea. It is a peculiar feeling to stand in the Tornillo Creek bed, which changes with every runoff, and look at land and oyster shells many millions of years old (Fig. 7.5).

Geology students might be interested in knowing that a giant clam shell measuring more than two feet across was found in this area. It was collected by geologist Ross Maxwell before he became Big Bend National Park's first superintendent. Ross displayed the clam shell in the CCC camp's museum of artifacts during the late 1930's, before the building was destroyed by fire.

Several of Big Bend's most priceless treasures are dinosaurs discovered in recent years. One of the first documented finds, in 1932, was in a cave at Mule Ears, where parts of three California condors were identi-

fied by Dr. A. Whetmore (Fig. 7.6). The bird dates back to the Pleis-
tocene epoch and is near extinction today. Other early finds include tur-
tle fragments, a primitive pantherlike cat, bones from the jaw of a tiny
camel, the dawn- (three-toed) horse, and other forest-dwelling mammals that have no modern counterpart.

In 1971, in the vicinity of Rattlesnake Mountain and Terlingua Creek,
geologists found the fossilized bones of a giant flying reptile, the pterodactyl. The wingspan of this prehistoric marvel measured an impressive
thirty-six to thirty-nine feet. It is the largest flying creature ever discovered. The long neck and head ended in a six-foot-long beak.[3]

Stop by the Visitor Center in Big Bend National Park or the
Museum of the Big Bend on the Sul Ross campus in Alpine to get an
idea of the pterodactyl's amazing size. The Texas Memorial Museum
[now the Texas Natural Science Center—Ed.] in Austin at one time
referred to the Big Bend pterodactyl as "the Big Flap" and has a display.
These museums have each mounted full-size replicas of the pterodactyl's
wing section to give the public a visual concept of its enormous size.

I do not know how many miles I have walked the desert looking for the
object of my constant dream—the skeleton of a woolly mammoth. During CCC days, a museum in the Basin displayed fossils of a mammoth
tusk and teeth found in the park by Dr. Ross Maxwell, so I know mammoths were here. Not long ago my hope was stimulated by a report that
a mammoth tusk deposited near the campfire of some early man had
been found, but the report was not substantiated. It does seem as though
a ten thousand–year–old mammoth would be easier to find than a seventy million–year–old *Alamosaurus*.

Somewhere in the Big Bend a mammoth surely walked into a lake or
marsh, became mired, died, and fell into the mud, where its skeletal
remains are preserved, waiting patiently through the millennia for me to
discover them.

The headwaters of Tornillo Creek begin in the area of Paint Gap Hills.
The hills are low and rocky with a heavy growth of grasses and shrubs.
This is attractive to foraging animals due to its proximity to nearby
Dripping Springs. Some animals and birds will allow the close approach

necessary for good wildlife pictures. Other creatures are timid. They hide in limited shadows or scoot swiftly across the sand, gravel, and rocks.

With camera ready and preset for distance and exposure, lucky grab shots are often possible; but a much better chance for success is to locate at a spring or water hole. This advantage still takes supreme patience—and luck—to achieve the quality of photos you envision. A blind would be the nearest thing to ideal for the cameraman but can be tragic for the birds and wildlife. When I first arrived in Big Bend I tried that but quit when I had a 100 percent loss on young birds, eggs, and, in some cases, small adult birds. Curious predators quickly spotted my location and wiped out the nests.

Wildlife photographers as a rule do not talk much about their work, and bird photographers even less. Most people do not understand the hard work, the patience, and the perseverance required. The only time you kind of let yourself go is when you meet another "nut" like yourself and trade stories. That makes all those lonely hours worthwhile.

A final word. When you show the results of your photographic work, don't expect too much enthusiasm as a result of your trouble.

Have you noticed the intensity with which all desert life survives? After a rain, the desert becomes another world. Vegetation is highly specialized in its ability to store and preserve water. Plants you have never seen in flower can rival those in our pampered gardens. A few days after a raging flood of water, you will see blossoms profusely scattered on the slopes above a dry wash. This is the benefit and miracle of moisture in a dry land. Photographers and artists have found the floral scenery of the desert with its unusual plants, erosional remnants, and open vistas a subject for their skill.

Notice that, while plants are widely spaced and seemingly alone, their survival depends on their neighbors. A rock—one you might want to cast into the arroyo—provides an environment which supports a plant, an insect, or perhaps a small mammal.

The Comanche Trail was a well-defined and hard-packed trail when seen by Hartz, Echols, and the camel expedition of 1859 on their way to the Rio Grande. The expedition followed the Chisos branch of the Indian trail through Cañón de Camello (now called Dog Canyon) near the Persimmon Gap entrance to Big Bend National Park. Dog Canyon carries the runoff from a very large area, so you would expect it to be a permanent stream, but this is not the case. Most of the rain is absorbed by the thirsty land before it gets there.

On Tornillo Flat, man's efforts to control the encroachment of arid desert was able to encourage grass and weeds to grow by pitting and breaking up the desert cement. In time, perhaps, Tornillo Flat will once again support a growth which old-timers say was belly-high to a horse (Fig. 7.7).

I have often walked the Comanche Trail and find it a worthwhile project for the backpacker, the photographer, or the inquisitive. If you have a desire to hike a historic trail which figured prominently in the life of early settlers, this is a good one to consider. Bill Cooper, who owned and operated Cooper's Store at Persimmon Gap [the building now serves as the east entrance station to the park—Ed.] directed me to Devil's Den in the 1940's. I explored it as a most scenic route to Dagger Flat.

Devil's Den is most easily reached where it is only a mile from the main road. By continuing up the draw and through the gap, one can reach the area where giant daggers (*Yucca carnerosana*) are most abundant. Thousands of these plants grow in the valleys and on the slopes of the Deadhorse Mountains. Some years, every plant within view produces a remarkable flowering stem with hundreds of blossoms. One bloom stalk I photographed measured seven feet nine inches. It was growing from a ten-foot plant and was a sight to see (Fig. 7.8).

Between Grapevine Hills and the Rosillos Mountains unusual, rounded, cementlike boulders are plentiful at the head of several draws. They range in size from cannonballs to those weighing many tons. In other areas, unusual layered shelves above the creek beds contain flat sandstone disks scattered in close formation, like stacks of pancakes or tortillas (Fig. 7.9).

Water in most of the major creeks shows up where the bedrock is exposed or pools form in deep depressions. On Tornillo Creek there are a number of such locations. After the park's establishment, water sources for game was a major concern. Most of the springs and water holes were recorded and watched for rate of flow.

Another section of the Tornillo watershed can be reached from the paved Boquillas road by hiking down Estufa Canyon. In 1946, this area included a swamp of considerable size. Cattails, swamp grasses, and clear pools of water dotted an area of about five acres. In 1976, the area

7.7. *As you walk the desert, look for these strange natural sculptures. With correct lighting you might capture a trophy like this rock I call Old Rattlesnake Rock. It is an erosional remnant overlooking Tornillo Creek, not far from Hot Springs.*

7.8. *Peter Koch self-portrait. Black Gap Wildlife Refuge to the east of the park has a display of* yucca rostrata *in the spring that rivals the display of giant daggers in the park.*

7.9. Here are a few of the rounded concretions that remained at the end of 1965. Several years before this, dozens of cannonball-sized concretions littered the area around the larger ones. It is only a matter of time until they are all gone.

was reduced by half, but cattails, grasses, and swamp-loving birds still gathered there.

Cattail ponds are a rarity in the Big Bend. Wherever their dense growth occurs you will likely find a place to see and photograph the uncommon wildfowl and marsh birds that are restricted to such wetlands.

Another photogenic area is Grapevine and an eroding rock formation I've always called Taj Mahal. It is found on Tornillo Flat about a half mile northwest of the Marathon road. A few desert plants, such as ocotillo, creosote, and several species of cactus, are spaced out among head-high boulders. These oddly shaped rocks add interest and improve the foreground of scenes toward the Chisos Mountains. Colorful vistas any time of year place this area at the top of my list (Fig. 7.10).

Beyond the Taj Mahal formation, another colorful rock can be seen poised above its steep slopes. The base of this formation is also worth exploring. It is a cave habitat of early man, who lived in the cool corridor and adjoining shelter. On top of the boulder overhanging the shelter are several deep bedrock mortars. Through the years they have accumulated windblown dirt and now serve as "flowerpots" for weeds. The view of the surrounding desert is unobstructed. Perhaps the overhang served as a watchtower to warn prehistoric man of an enemy approaching the shelter (Fig. 7.11).

In a shallow cave between the large boulders is a mass of flakes, chips, and unfinished artifacts, which indicates that this was a workshop in which men fashioned their lithic tools. Only a portion of it is exposed.

Facing the Chisos Mountains and slightly to the right of Pulliam Peak is another sculpture. I refer to this desert formation as the "Phoenix" because of its similarity to the old legend's bird figure towering above the mesa—the ashes.

Halfway between the Taj Mahal and the Phoenix, hidden in stunted mesquite, are several dozen circular rock middens called sotol pits. Sotol

7.10. Taj Mahal lies about half a mile from the Persimmon Gap entrance road. The walk, toward the north, is on a flat desert floor. Desert plants, such as ocotillo, creosote, and several species of cactus, may be found among the head-high boulders.

7.11. This cave on Tornillo Creek has a magnificent view of the rock sculptures seen as you enter the park on Highway 385 from Marathon.

pits are identified on the desert by the rocks which encircle them. Archeologists explain that the depressions were made in the earth to create a pit. Wood was added and a roaring fire was built. Rocks were thrown into the fire and heated until they were extremely hot. At that point, the wood ashes were removed and agave or sotol hearts were placed in the pit with the heated rocks. They were then covered with earth and left to cook for several days. When the fire pit had cooled, the plants were removed and eaten or dried and ground into flour.[4]

Other tools were used in food preparation. The metate and mano are an example. A metate is a smooth, flat stone slab. The mano is the grinding stone, held in the hand like an elongated bar of soap. Grass or plant seeds placed on the metate and rubbed with the mano will be ground into meal, or flour, which will be cooked or stored. In time, the metate becomes worn into a most-treasured shallow rectangular, bowl-shaped utensil (Fig. 7.12).

The Indians, who lived on the banks of Tornillo, no doubt left their home and hunting grounds when there was a show of military force in the 1870's. I believe the Indians left quickly, for at principal camps a number of metates and manos were left behind. Such valued tools would have been carried away had there been time.

Tornillo Creek is, without question, for its entire length the most interesting of all streams included in the park. The variety of scenery, spacious vistas, numerous concentrations of varicolored boulders, groves of yuccas, and colorful desert flowers, combined with a relatively easy hiking terrain, can be enjoyed at any season (Fig. 7.13).

I believe a thorough exploration of Tornillo is necessary if you really want to know and understand the Big Bend desert. Although many changes have occurred in the needs of man, who is an inseparable part of the land he occupies, we must treat the land—especially the desert—with care and respect.

Enjoy your time on Tornillo Creek. Perhaps *you* will be the lucky one to discover the bones of that woolly mammoth.

7.12. In this location, an Indian maiden kneeled to grind seeds gathered from some of the native grasses. The mesquite tree has long since lost its leaves and beans, which provided food for some of the migrant food-gathering tribes living in the Big Bend. An extremely heavy rain washed away the soil which covered the metate and mano.

7.13. Tornillo Creek, without question, is the most interesting of all streams in the park.

MY HOT SPRINGS FLOOD STORY

by Patricia Koch

Dad gave me a pile of dishes. "Now you take these down to the creek and wash them," he said in a tone that must naturally be obeyed when you are only ten years old.

Why hadn't Dad washed the dishes as usual? Had I forgotten my daily chore of hauling two buckets of water from the well? I hated the job of scraping dried egg off the plates with sand and pebbles. But who could argue with Dad?

I lugged the aluminum ware in a bucket through the burning sand to Tornillo Creek and had just made myself comfortable on the creek bank and begun the disagreeable job when I was surprised by a wall of water coming right at me.

"Help!" I gasped and scrambled up the bank to safety as the pots and pans floated happily toward the Rio Grande.

I ran back to the store to tell Dad the news and suggest that we needed to buy replacements right away. But only a few moments later, the pans reappeared. Some campers near the river risked being swept away by the floodwater in order to save and return to us our dirty dishes.

Later that summer another flood occurred while we were swim-ming in the river with some friends. Suddenly, there were alarming shouts from the bank and a general roar as branches and boulders came tumbling toward us at the point where the creek and river met.

Someone waded into the water with a long tow rope, which we all grabbed for safety. Our footing was no match for the shifting sands, but we struggled against the water's force and were pulled ashore through the rocks and branches as we watched the water eat away at the bank. It was an eerie feeling, indeed.

WORKING WITH WARNOCK

*P*lease be considerate of those who have yet to visit the
Big Bend. Keep the park clean. Leave wildflowers, trees,
animals, rocks, and natural features as you find them.
And remember! It is not wise to pet the rattlesnakes.

Peter Koch

AN ENGLISH NATURALIST once spoke to a group of Ohio
Scouts of which I was a member. He suggested that more natural history
could be learned by studying a square yard of earth than could be
learned on a fourteen-mile hike.

Intrigued, we boys gathered around his chosen square yard of soil,
and I listened spellbound as he described life on this earth when the
limestone pebble he held in his hand was formed. Each rock, each
insect, beetle, and spider that wandered into the square became an actor
in his drama of life on this planet. He spoke of life in the sea, freshwater
lakes, ponds and streams, glaciers, marshes, and forests. He spoke of
their changes during eons, from early geologic ages to the present day.
He named every bird that passed overhead and identified each sound we
heard. He emphasized the need for observation and an inquisitive
nature.

Only one other person in my life has opened the door to nature's
miracles as did this man from England. This was Dr. Barton H.
Warnock, chairman of the Biology Department at Sul Ross State University. For two years he and I worked together to photograph the flowers of the Trans-Pecos.

My work with Barton was preceded by a request from Harold W.
Rickett of the New York Botanical Garden to provide photographs for
their books of the flowering plants of Texas (published by them in

1969–70). I was pleased that over one hundred of my transparencies were selected to appear in the two Texas volumes.[1]

Barton had planned for many years to publish three wildflower books. One each for the Big Bend and Guadalupe Mountains, and a third for the Davis Mountains and Marathon Basin.[2]

Together Barton and I searched the niches in canyons, mountains, and plains where he knew a certain flower made its home. He knew when plants were at their very best and rarely missed the opening day of a new flower.

Barton handed me a small magnifying hand lens one day and said, "Pete, you really should *see* what you are filming." I immediately discovered I had never really seen a daisy. I had never really seen grass flowers either, until I viewed the amazing tiny flowers with a hand lens. You should try it sometime.

Many trips with Barton began with a strenuous mountain climb. Beyond the deciduous trees and above the shaded boulders we found rocks covered with colorful yellow, orange, and gray lichens. Flowers and plants were found in the dry ground of steep slopes or, like miniature gardens, hanging from the giant boulders.

On the highest slopes and mountains in Texas we found pristine grassy basins and took time to check carefully for flowers hidden within the rimrock cracks. When the wind was uncomfortable or the rain beat down with force, we found shelter. A small discomfort forgotten at day's end when we counted twenty, thirty, sometimes forty plants found and successfully photographed.

A major event happened one day at the top of Mount Livermore in the Davis Mountains. We stopped to rest on a patch of grass and Barton nearly sat on a small annual herb, thereby discovering a new plant species. He named it *Sisyrinchium powellii* in honor of another biologist at Sul Ross [most likely A. Michael Powell—Ed.].

Until I worked with Barton, I didn't know that at least five orchid species could be found in the Chisos Mountains. I photographed one he found which had a bloom only a half-inch long. It represented an orchid Barton had never before seen in the park.

There are over two thousand West Texas plant species. Of all the wildflowers indigenous to Texas, about 50 percent are found in the nine-county Trans-Pecos area. When you consider that the Trans-Pecos region represents only 12 percent of the land area in Texas, you can understand the importance of this country to botanists.[3]

There are many interesting features about the familiar plants in our area. I thought you might like to have a few of these facts to share with your relatives when they come visiting or to casually mention to a friend you want to impress as you show them your photographs.

The ocotillo (*Fouquieria splendens*) plant is the most interesting, I think, and like many other desert residents I look forward each spring to the sight of the ocotillo's flame-colored blossoms decorating the tip of each crooked, leafy stem. The ocotillo was once described to me by a visitor as a bunch of fifteen- to twenty-foot wiggly snakes tied together at the neck, with their heads stuck in the ground. Well—maybe so—at least I knew exactly which plant he was talking about.

The panicles of bright scarlet blossoms appear at the tip of each ocotillo stalk in late April or May and are at their best for about three or four weeks. Small leaves appear after a rain and are shed during the dry period that follows. I also learned the thorny stalks will root if they are "planted" close together in the ground and held in place with woven rope or wire. The resulting patio or pen will continue to leaf and bloom each year after the early summer rains.

Barton said the pioneers used ocotillo fences to keep the coyotes away from the chickens. I suppose people along the Rio Grande have had flowering fences for untold centuries. The idea that those contorted, heavily thorned, dead-looking sticks contained such magic was something I'd never imagined in my pre–Big Bend years.

Not long after my arrival in the park, I was in the Tornillo desert filming ocotillo when I noticed—through the lens of my camera—that the flowers which had fallen on the ground were in motion. Upon inspection I discovered a confusion of ants hoisting the blooms as best they could and carrying them off across the hot desert to their cool subterranean nests. What a stunning movie scene it created when I showed the close-up film of the ants' activity! It certainly got my theater audience's attention.

When the ocotillo begins to bloom, watch for the hummingbirds' arrival. Their migration seems timed precisely with the opening of the ocotillo buds and the bloom of other red flowers.

The flowering period for ocotillo in the lower desert ends in early May, but the progression continues, ascending upward into the foothills and mountain slopes. The hummingbirds follow the bloom until they find a suitable nesting place at the appropriate time.

Other red flowers attractive to hummingbirds and insects are the low shrubs of bouvardia (*Bouvardia ternifolia*) and salvia (*Salvia regla*). These plants, from three to six feet high, are frequently loaded with narrow, tubular scarlet flowers. The showy plants are easy to spot along the road-side in the upper Green Gulch and in the Basin.

Maguey (*Agave scabra* or *Agave havardiana*) is commonly called century plant. In spite of the name, these plants do not take a hundred years to mature and bloom. They complete their life cycle in about twenty years. After they bloom the leaves and the stalk die, but many young plants are waiting for their turn to rise and shine. The century plant bloom stalk grows quickly—as much as twelve to fifteen feet in just a few days. It looks like a monumental stalk of asparagus until the "branches" form and the yellow tubelike flowers open. This plant's dead bloom stalks are the ones I used to build the raft for my float trip through Santa Elena Canyon. Indians roasted many parts of this plant for food. Pulque, an alcoholic drink made in Mexico, is also made from this plant.

Did you know that yuccas are members of the lily family? They display their spectacular blooms early in the year. The spine-tipped leaves protect the luxuriant cluster of ivory lilylike flowers on stalks sprouting from the center of the spines. The soaptree yucca (*Yucca elata*) is a good indicator of grassland overutilization, because young plants take over when the native grasses are removed. It often forms a single- or multi-headed plant. Barton says the yucca flowers may be eaten raw in a salad or made into preserves.

Giant daggers (*Yucca carnerosana*) are the largest variety. They grow to a height of fifteen to twenty feet and are topped by a bloom that measures up to seven feet above the large, flat, spine-tipped leaves. An extraordinary year at Dagger Flat brings more than ten thousand plants into flower. Spring is a prime time for you to visit, photograph, and enjoy Dagger Flat.

The Indians were highly dependent upon the yucca plants. They collected the fruits of the *Yucca torreyi* and stored them in shelters. (Barton thinks the ripe fruits taste like applesauce.) There are six species of yuccas in our area and not all of them are edible, so *be sure* before you taste.

Yucca fiber has been a source for making ropes, baskets, and shoes for centuries. The roots and stems of some varieties were also used to make soap.

I hope someday soon a knowledgeable person will devote time to studying our edible desert plants. I guess I should also try one of those big juicy grasshoppers. I expect it would be an experience to remember.

An abundantly good year, about one in twenty, brings an annual rainfall of sixteen to twenty inches to this country. When drenching rains fall during September, October, or November, the hard seeds of bluebonnets (*Lupinus havardii*) and other biennial plants begin to germinate. The result—a spectacular spring exhibition on every hillside and desert flat. Wet areas such as sandy arroyos and rocky slopes along the roadsides encourage our West Texas species of bluebonnet to grow to exceptional size, three to four feet high, in many cases. Windblown seeds, or those carried by rodents to shelters under protecting rocks, will root and sprout. Most will reach maturity and complete their life cycle. The floral display of bluebonnets at Black Gap Wildlife Management Area often rivals the beauty of the giant daggers at Dagger Flat. If you collect seeds of the bluebonnet, plant them in the fall. They flower best in rainy years between January and June.

The ceniza's (*Leucophyllum frutescens* or *Leucophyllum violaceum*) rose purple flowers beautify our roadsides and mountain slopes with the delicate colors of spring. Looking at the ceniza in bloom reminds me of the Smoky Mountains and the slow drizzle and fog that usher in the rose purple rhododendron each spring.

The ceniza buds appear three or four days after a good rain. About ten days later the plant produces a miracle of pink, violet purple, or blue flowers. You can burn up a lot of color film at such times. There is no doubt that the lower Green Gulch area is at its best when the ceniza blooms. The delicate flowers, with an opalescent haze on distant peaks, or as a foreground for swirling mountain fog, spell renewal and rebirth.

The display of pitaya (*Echinocereus stramineus*) or strawberry cactus, in the Tornillo watershed is worth traveling miles to see (Fig. 8.1). The gray mound-shaped pitaya plant grows in clusters of up to several feet in diameter, and after its purplish red blossoms wither away, it produces an edible fruit. If the loose spines of the fruit are removed and the outer skin is peeled away like a banana, a dull pinkish gray fruit speckled with small black seeds is revealed. The fruit tastes like a cross between strawberries and raspberries—delicious on ice cream or sliced into a bowl with sugar and cream.

Around Alpine and the Davis Mountains, variously colored chollas (*Opuntia imbricata* and *Opuntia kleiniae*) are prevalent. They range from apple blossom pink to deep reddish plum in color. The cholla and the abundantly common prickly pear mark the end of the cactus flowering season. The Indians cooked the fruits of these plants in rock-lined pits or sun dried them. The fruits of both chollas and prickly pears are thought to be high in calcium.

On one photo trip in the Redford area, Warnock showed me several

8.1. *The pitaya was probably the most popular plant with early residents of the Big Bend. After the blossoms whither away, an edible fruit is produced that tastes similar to strawberries or raspberries.*

unusual plants growing in a side canyon. One I remember vividly was Cory's dutchman's pipe (*Aristolochia coryi*). This unusual plant finds a hold in earth-filled cracks on mountain cliffsides. Its small, modestly colored flowers bloom in the shape of a gentleman's pipe. This herb belongs to a large tropical forest family, all bearing strange, pipe-shaped blooms. To find two species in this isolated canyon is further evidence that the Big Bend at one time had a forested environment.

A few words about the lechuguilla (*Agave lechuguilla*) are essential, since it is the indicator plant—and probably the most prolific resident—of the Chihuahuan Desert. Lechuguilla is a plant folks try to avoid, for, in its favored limestone location, it grows so thickly that traveling through the ankle-deep thorny challenge can be difficult if not impossible. It is not kind to the ankles of cattle or horses either. The points break off and are very painful, sometimes crippling the animal. Indians used fiber from the green banana-shaped leaves to make ropes, baskets, and mats. They also distilled intoxicants by fermenting the sap.

I remember one year in which the lechuguilla in the park bloomed so profusely around Dugout Wells on the Hot Springs road, it was difficult to see the Sierra del Carmen through the abundance of flowering stalks. I remember it because I was running short of film and made a note to be better prepared the following year. Well, I have never again seen a display to match it.

A plant's means of survival develops slowly over countless years. Some species are shallow rooted and sprout from seeds a day or so after a rain, to live, mature, and die in a matter of a week or so. Others, like the resinous creosote bush (*Larrea tridentata*), survive because of a very extensive network of roots so close to the surface that they deter growth by any rival plant. In Mary Austin's *Land of Little Rain* I read that Indians used a scale found on creosote branches as a glue for mending pottery, attaching arrow points, and waterproofing baskets.

Many people erroneously call this plant "greasewood"; others refer to it as hediondilla, which means "little stinker." (If you crush—and smell—the leaves, you will agree.) The flowers are small and yellow. The fruits look like small fuzzy balls. The pleasant fragrance of the plants after a good rain makes creosote a desert highlight you'll never forget.

Creosote is the abundant green-leaved shrub that occurs almost everywhere in the desert. Its very small leaves are covered with a resinous material that restricts evaporation, another of this plant's adaptations for desert survival.[4]

Honey mesquite (*Prosopis glandulosa*) is among those plants which bloom profusely in the spring. The mesquite beans that follow are as long as, but lumpier than, string beans and they are edible. I've heard they can be chewed raw but have never tried it. Livestock, particularly cattle, eat the leaves and fruits. It was a staple in the diet of many Indians. Excellent jelly is made from ripe pods, which have a high sugar content. Mesquite is not a plant you want to brush against while hiking (or get dumped into while checking panther caves), since every branch is armed with long, pointed thorns that are not obvious until they jab you.

In well-watered areas mesquite grows into a graceful tree. The roots of mesquite and others of the acacia or mimosa family send their roots as far as 150 feet down into the earth for life-giving moisture. The smoke from a mesquite wood fire is of "gourmet quality" and offers a distinctive taste to barbecue dinners as well as desert campfires in the Southwest. Mesquite is a hardwood and has been used for fence posts and furniture for many years.

Another small, attractive tree is the desert willow (*Chilopsis linearis*).

You will see it growing abundantly in the Big Bend along arroyos and mountain streams. The pinkish purple flowers remind me of small orchids. The desert willow blooms after the summer rains. The seeds are easy to germinate, and this tree is a pleasant addition to many southwestern gardens.

Many areas make much of their flowering season, but if we consider the variety, abundance, and beauty of these—and countless other plants—we stand with the very best.

The miracle of life in the desert is a wondrous thing. Here we find a plant so fragile in appearance one would expect the intense heat of the sun to burn the petals to a crisp and the wind to rip and tear the slender-stemmed blossoms from their roots. Yet these brilliant blossoms seem to be affected but slightly. At moments when every condition is just right, swarms of insects appear magically and visit the plants to perform the necessary chore of carrying the life-giving pollen to stigmas where they will eventually fertilize the seeds that assure next year's crop. This goes on in city gardens, of course, but somehow it seems to be more of a miracle here in the desert, where the cycle of life is more readily seen in an area easily scanned and with few factors to distract us.

During the summer of 1946, when I filmed the documentary *Desert Gold*, I accented the golden colors of the desert ranchland. In one movie sequence I filmed the flat grasslands around Marathon, which at the time was an amazing expanse of gold that undulated across the countryside. I then photographed other flowers in intimate detail, such as the huge yellow blossoms of the rainbow or hedgehog cactus (*Echinocereus dasyacanthus*). I also included golden grasshoppers, tree toads, and birds, such as yellow-headed blackbirds and Scott's oriole. The photographs and story line of the documentary pleased me, since I was a relative newcomer to the area.

The film's success was confirmed in 1953, when Mr. Erwin L. Verity, then in charge of Disney Nature Productions, patterned the company's well-known movie *The Living Desert* after my film. (Disney's production team studied the film during three of my showings at the Chicago Natural History Museum and adapted my storytelling style and film techniques to their production.)

The wonders of time-lapse photography, close-ups, and macrophotography and many sophisticated photographic devices, such as are used in the production of TV nature spectaculars, is one dramatic way of stirring up an appreciation of the natural scene.

The reason I mention this is to stress that the Big Bend–Davis

Mountains area is an area outstanding in a variety of concepts. My film and Disney's both focused on the amazing qualities to be found in the desert. The desert is exceptional in its earth science and unique history, the strong character of its people, and its authentic Old West charm.

Barton once joined me in a hike in the vicinity of Elephant Tusk mountain. Neither of us had been in the area before. Our objective was to reach a historic Indian campsite located in that area. I was focused on the objective, but Warnock found every hill and rock-strewn valley we entered interesting. He was alert to any item which would show this area to be different from the surrounding country.

I was wearing myself out with frustration at Warnock's meandering enjoyment. When we came to a moist canyon where vegetation was lush and concentrated in a lovely sunken garden, I gave up the idea of reaching the prehistoric site. It was past midday, and we were five miles from the parked car in country described by Lieutenant Hartz in his report as a journey of "very steep slopes into the bed of ravines, tumbling about for a while among the rocks in their beds, climbing up steep hillsides, [and] forcing a way through thickets."

It was in the vegetation of the lush sunken garden that Warnock found a screech owl asleep in a shallow tunnel. With camera ready, I asked Barton to capture the owl and hold it for a picture. The owl wanted to be secure in his perch and fastened its talons into Barton's hand. Releasing the owl was more difficult than the capturing of it. It took the efforts of both of us to unfasten each talon without gouging a bit of flesh from his hand.

After the tiring effort of reaching the dead-end canyon and the experience with the owl, neither of us had the energy or the inclination to climb out of the canyon toward the flat area where the camp was said to be located. With disappointment I followed him back to the car.

I'm sorry to say I never did have an opportunity to return to the area to film the historic site.

Take time to visit the fine collection of Trans-Pecos plants at the Sul Ross State University herbarium when you are in Alpine. Barton Warnock and other botanists spent years gathering these plants for study purposes.

Time is also wisely spent at the Barton Warnock Environmental

Education Center near Lajitas. This facility was established in 1982 in part to honor Warnock's sixty years of research on plants of the Chihuahuan Desert.

THE SINGLE BLOOMING FLOWER

by Don Dhonau

On our first or second day [in Alpine], Pete said he had to drive to the desert, fifty or sixty miles toward the park, to photograph a flower that blooms only a few hours in its entire life.

"It is about that time!" he said.

I asked if I could go with him and he said I could, if I realized that we would have to spend the night in the desert sleeping on the ground. I agreed and off we went, driving at full speed down the highway. Much of the desert looks the same, especially at sixty miles an hour and at dusk. Pete talked very little, but all at once he came to a stop saying, "Here we are."

I thought to myself, "Here we are where? There is nothing here except what we have been driving past for the last hour."

By the time we found "less rocky" ground and laid out our sleeping bags, it was dark and we went to bed. It was so dark I could see nothing. It was so quiet that the ticking of my watch at arm's length threatened to keep me awake. We heard the occasional wail of the coyotes, and I was a bit apprehensive, but I survived until morning. Pete had no trouble sleeping.

When I was awakened by the daylight, Pete was already up. We walked some distance from our "campsite" directly to the location of a single blooming flower, no more than twelve to fourteen inches high and maybe in diameter the size of a quarter. All this way, this far off the road, and Pete knew exactly where it was and when he needed to be there to film it—the right light, the right time, the right place. . . . Pete was a man of precision, of detail, of single-mindedness, consumed by his love of the natural world.

To me, as a person who was "familiar" with his world but not fully a part of it, the whole episode was remarkable!

PRESIDIO COUNTY

*M*an always kills the things he loves, and so we the pioneers have killed our wilderness. Some say we had to. Be that as it may, I am glad I shall never be young without wild country to be young in.

Aldo Leopold

NAMES LIKE CHINATI, Candelaria, and Capote have an exotic quality that sounds like adventure. So if you are looking for something out of the ordinary and are in the mood to explore, take the loop trip from Marfa to the Rio Grande (see Map 5). This is an especially good outing for the winter months, as the lower desert can get pretty hot on a summer day. Part of the road is primitive, but safe. You may drive all the way to Ruidosa without meeting a car, so it is "lonesome land." I suggest driving a counterclockwise loop. You will find it offers the best views of Pinto Canyon and Chinati Mountain.

Early-day tourists visiting the Big Bend were commonly called "waterbaggers" because of the canvas water bags and coolers hanging from various extensions of the car. Now the popular mode of travel is with the kitchen sink and refrigerator in a camper or RV.

Our county roads are maintained for safe travel with interpretive devices and pamphlets to explain what you will be seeing. It is best to think like a good Scout and "be prepared." At one of the service stations in Marfa, prepare your vehicle by checking tires and water and filling the gas tank. You might want to stock up on a few snacks, extra water, and film. (This is always a good idea whenever you start into the "outback.")

Before you leave Marfa, take time to drive around the historic courthouse north of the railroad tracks. Presidio County has hosted many movie crews throughout the years. It should probably be considered the "movie capital of West Texas."

One of the most famous movies, *Giant*, was filmed in the summer and fall of 1955 and created quite a local stir. Rock Hudson, Elizabeth Taylor, and James Dean stayed in town and used the Paisano Hotel as their headquarters. The stars kept the local telephone operators titillated with their late-night phone calls. *Giant* is a story about a land- and oil-rich Texas family and is based on Edna Ferber's book of that name.

When you are ready to leave town for your trip to Presidio, return to the midtown traffic light on Highway 90. Drive west a few blocks to the junction of FM 2810 and turn south. This is the road to Pinto Canyon and Ruidosa. The first portion of the road is paved, and on either side of the road are large ranches typical of the ranch in *Giant*. These ranches are among the best in our mile-high grasslands. The elevation at Pinto

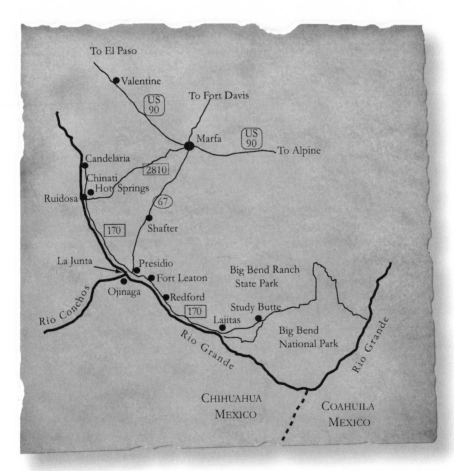

5. Presidio County

9.1. The Pinto Canyon road is one of spectacular vistas and subtle desert colors. Views from the top or bottom portray a lonesome land.

Canyon summit, where the paved road ends, is about fifty-two hundred feet (Fig. 9.1).

Slow down at the top of the hill and test your brakes to be sure they will hold. Shift into low gear and drive slow down the steep grade into Pinto Canyon. You'll want to drive slowly enough to take an occasional look at the spectacular landscape below. The road descends about eight hundred feet, and several turnout places are suitable for parking. *Never* park on the narrow road or stop, even momentarily, at a turn. If you are one of those people who depend on an accident to learn, this is a good place. The twenty-mile walk for help will give you sufficient time to think about your mistake.

As you start down the hill, the spectacular vistas and the subtle variety of desert colors will absorb your attention. You will soon arrive at a Shangri-La, Big Bend's "High Lonesome."

High Lonesome is the name of the great western starring John Drew

Barrymore and Chill Wills that was filmed here in 1950. The perlite mine was not developed then, but beyond the mine to the right are several adobe buildings. This is all that is left of the home ranch in the story.

Chinati Mountain, colorful hills, and rocky outcroppings provide the backdrop for a mysterious, isolated ranch. On the road below the adobes is the very narrow "shotgun pass" that still provides the sensation of entering a forbidden land.

A word about good manners in the outback is appropriate. The area may seem to be completely abandoned, but these are working ranches. Get permission if you want to explore. (Finding the owner is not always easy and should be done in Marfa.)

Do Not Trespass! Identify yourself and always leave a note in the car explaining where you are going and why. Leave gates as you find them, and *please* don't litter!

Several years ago I climbed Chinati Mountain, elevation seventy-seven hundred feet. I was searching for a rare orchid named for Barton Warnock—*Hexalectris warnockii*—one of the Big Bend's most delicate. The climb was long and hot, but from the high elevations the scenery was spectacular. The vegetation was more abundant than I've found on other Big Bend mountains except, perhaps, Mount Livermore.

Many species of perennials and annuals were in flower, but I did not find the orchid, probably because I was overwhelmed by the magnificent vistas stretching in every direction a hundred miles and more. "High Lonesome" is also the perfect description of Chinati Mountain. It would be an ideal place to spend some time exploring or examining the flora more closely. It is a place to be alone accompanied only by isolation, solitude, and contemplation. If the confusion of a regimented world has been too much for you, look around at this isolated world where trouble, confusion, and regimentation do not exist.

Farther along you will reach a steep grade leading to a long ridge that eventually brings you to Ruidosa and FM 170. Turn right on the paved road and stop at the Ruidosa store. The store is usually open and refreshments are available. Stop in and get acquainted with the owners. They are friendly, well informed, and glad to answer your questions.

Take time to walk over to the abandoned church, the Mission of the Sacred Heart of Jesus. It is of historic vintage (built in 1914) and typical of old mission architecture. It is worthwhile to stand quietly near the

9.2. *Rapidly deteriorating early mission ruins can be found along FM 170. Some years ago, this area was plowed and a ceramic figure of Christ was recovered. For many years, the small statue occupied a niche beside an entrance to the chapel. Portions of the altar and decorations were still in this adobe building when it was photographed.*

adobe ruins and imagine a Sunday morning years ago when people from miles around arrived in wagons or on burros or horseback and filled the church. More than a thousand people were living in the area at that time. Many worked on cotton farms or at one of several cotton gins.[1]

It is believed that the Rio Grande all the way from Candelaria to Boquillas was heavily populated for centuries. Most were farmers who lived where substantial arable land was available. They located near the Rio Grande or on tributaries which had sufficient seasonal runoff to provide subsoil moisture and water for irrigation (Fig. 9.2).

Estimates for the population vary considerably, but from the number of ruins it must have been well up in the thousands. Campsites and caves tell us the area, which seems to be vast and lonely, has been occupied since prehistoric times.[2]

From Ruidosa you can, and should, continue upriver to Chinati Hot Springs and Candelaria, the ultimate in rustic and remote sites in this part of the desert. Turn north on the dirt road "around the corner" from

9.3. Many dramatic formations in the Big Bend are composed of volcanic ash deposited after the eruptions which formed the Rocky Mountains. Ashes blanketed the Southwest. Water erosion and floods washed the ashes into depressions, where they were saturated with lime and other minerals to form a cemented material called tuff.

Ruidosa. It is only about four miles to Chinati Hot Springs. The buildings, for the most part, were built back in the 1930's, when it was known as Kingston Hot Springs. The oasis still retains the flavor of pioneer times. Rooms, a campground (sorry, there are no RV spaces), and a picnic area are available, and the warm mineral baths are reputed to "cure everything but laziness." If you are interested in solitude and a good location for bird-watching and wildlife photography, you will enjoy your stop at Chinati Hot Springs. [The Chinati Hot Springs have been modernized but are still considered a peaceful, rustic oasis for those who are looking for relief from the stresses of life in our hysterical world.—Ed.]

Candelaria is about ten miles upriver from Ruidosa. The approach is marked by a conspicuious geologic formation on the Mexican side called a "*pilón*" [tuff spires] (Fig. 9.3). Perched side by side on a rise above Candelaria some years ago were the church, the school, and the jail. What a neighborly way of impressing young students with the results of their good—or bad—conduct.

The village of Candelaria is now a quiet community in an area often described as desolate by writers who have not learned to see in a spacious desert country. They have not been away from trees long enough to see the unique desert vegetation, the dramatic landforms, and the variety of delicate colors in vast spaciousness.

Just past Candelaria is "the end of the road." Some years ago, the landowners permitted access to Capote Falls, but to my knowledge it is no longer open without prior permission from the owners (Fig. 9.4).

After you backtrack on FM 170 to Ruidosa and Presidio, you have a choice. You can continue toward Lajitas and Study Butte, spend the night in Presidio, or turn north on US 67 at the highway junction in Presidio and return to Marfa. I highly recommend driving to Lajitas and returning to Presidio. This way you will have two opportunities to travel the Camino del Río highway. A national highway contest listed it as one of the ten most spectacular drives in the United States, so you really should see it twice.

The roadway constitutes a marvel of engineering construction. It is carved from stone and plunges through deep canyons and through a most scenic area. The farm road designation may be misleading, for the modern highway is superbly built and equals many primary roads in the state. Large RV's, however, may have difficulty climbing Big Hill.

Lieutenant Echols and the camels arrived in Presidio on July 17, 1860, after his journey south along Alamito Creek from Fort Davis. Echols must have been hot and in a grouchy mood the night he wrote this in his journal:

> Made visits to the city on the 18th and 19th: called on the alcalde. Saw a great deal of the place, but found little worth seeing. All the buildings are of adobe, and present much the same appearance of a large dirt-dauber's nest. The population is about 3,100 according to the alcalde; but about half, or less, are a den of thieves. . . . The alcalde came into camp and spent about an hour, admiring the

camels . . . We have been trying to employ a guide ever since our
arrival at Presidio del Norte and only succeeded in obtaining one
today after we left camp. I hear they work for 25 cents a day with
rations and 37.5 without but would not hire to us for two dollars a
day and rations; [I learned] most of them are afraid we will hang
them, and were anxious to be paid in advance.[3]

Historians believe Cabeza de Vaca and his companions were the first
European visitors to wander into La Junta (Presidio-Ojinaga), about
1535. The Indians, known as the Jumano, were at that time well settled
along the Rio Grande and the Río Conchos (Fig. 9.5).

The Spaniards recorded that the Jumano were a farming rather than
a nomadic community and that they raised corn, beans, and squash in
small plots along the river.

The Jumano were a combination of several tribes gathered here for
mutual protection against warlike tribes and had blended into a new culture. As one community they established trade with other villages along
the Río del Norte and the Río Conchos and continued to farm the valley of La Junta. They tended their crops and obediently accepted the
benefits of Catholicism as taught by the missionaries who appeared
from time to time. The Jumano took Christian names but, being a practical people, they continued to worship their ancient gods as well. The
presence and policies of the missions, padres, and their presidio-forts
rose and declined for three hundred years according to the whims of the
Spanish authorities, the slave traders, and the ferocity of Apache and
Comanche invaders.

Mexico won its War of Independence in 1821, thus ending Spanish
rule; however, Texas remained a part of Mexico until 1836, when it
became an independent republic. (Texas did not become part of the
United States until 1845.)

·In spite of Apache and Comanche raids, trade routes were established between the United States and Mexico. In the 1830's, long wagon
trains of from ten to fifty wagons snaked their way across the plains
between Independence, Missouri, and Santa Fe, New Mexico. At Santa

*9.4. The 170-foot drop of Capote Falls is fed by a spring on private land in southern
Presidio County. It is a magnificent and rare symbol of what may have been a common sight twelve thousand years ago.*

9.5. Quite a few years ago, it was necessary to cross the Río Conchos, just south of its confluence with the Rio Grande, on a very primitive bridge.

Fe they turned south and continued to El Paso, then another 150 miles south of the Rio Grande to Ciudad Chihuahua.

In the late 1840's, some of the freighters also determined that a shorter route would be to cross the Big Bend Country by following the Río Conchos from Ciudad Chihuahua to La Junta, then trail up Alamito Creek north to Paisano Pass [between Marfa and Alpine—Ed.]. By continuing northeast they could reach the Pecos River and eventually St. Louis. Or they could follow the Chihuahua Trail [the "highway of horror" mentioned in Chap. 3—Ed.] from the Pecos River east to San Antonio, Victoria, Indianola, and the Gulf of Mexico by following several chains of well-known springs and water holes.

Probably the first Anglo freighters/traders to settle in Presidio after the war with Mexico were J. W. Spencer, J. D. Burgess, Ben Leaton, and Milton Faver. Spencer settled on land he called Spencer's Rancho and developed a horse ranch on land now occupied by the town of Presidio.

Burgess developed a major freighting company with headquarters at Spencer's Rancho. Burgess's trade goods included products made from paper, iron, fabric, and glass; candles; tobacco; and champagne, all of which he exchanged in Mexico for gold and silver bullion from the Mexican mines, buffalo rugs, furs, and longhorn cattle.

Milton Faver moved farther north and established his far-reaching cattle ranch near Shafter.

Ben Leaton was well qualified for the title of pioneer, trader, rancher, and (at times) scalp hunter. He somehow managed to obtain rights to a Mexican land grant that covered 2,345 square miles (1.5 million acres) of land.

Presidio County at that time included all land in Texas west of the Pecos River. The first seat of justice for unorganized Presidio County was located at Leaton's ranch.

Leaton, probably in 1848, began building his forty-room adobe fort and trading post four miles east of Presidio on the north side of the river. It was large enough to include quarters for his entire family, employees, and guests. It even sheltered within its walls his entire remuda of saddle horses to protect them from Indian raids.

Lieutenant Echols and the camels stopped at the fort to visit with Leaton on their way to Presidio. Echols's diary entry of July 17, 1860, records that he "reached Fort Leaton 4.1 miles from town—an old ranche [sic] established for a trading post etc, on a grant from the Mexican government . . . Stopped to dine with Mr. Leaton, and had a magnificient dinner, and abundance of water melons; plenty of them and musk melons in the vicinity."[4]

Early freighters were frequent visitors here in the mid-1800's as they traveled between San Antonio and Ciudad Chihuahua, Mexico, 150 miles south of Presidio. The earliest freighters used thick-wheeled wooden carts they called "*carretas*." You can see a *carreta* when visiting Fort Leaton. The solid wooden wheels are five to six feet in diameter, and, I'm told, were quite squeaky. It is said that women walked beside the wheels and greased them with twigs from the creosote bush as they traveled.[5]

The history of Fort Leaton is quite dramatic and filled with mystery and colorful legends. It is well worth your time to stop and visit this historic park.

As you drive comfortably on the roadway that winds along the floodplain linking small, picturesque river villages, notice the fields still being cultivated and nourished by the waters of the Rio Grande and the Río Conchos. Consider the long history and the enduring people of La Junta de los Ríos (the Junction of the Rivers), whose Jumano ancestors

9.6. There is a diversity of rocks in the Big Bend Country. Scrambled throughout the area are flagstones, cobblestones, volcanic ash, and igneous boulders. A photographic delight!

lived peacefully in this fertile valley. Today, as we travel east and west of Presidio along the curving river we call the Rio Grande, remember that your footprints—and your presence—will also be written in the wind-blown sands.

Big Bend Ranch and the Solitario extend from Redford to Lajitas, and the dramatic mountain scenery seen from the roadside is but a sample of their beauty. My only suggestion is to slow down. The Rio Grande is to your right, and a few Mexican villages can be seen adjacent to farms and river cane across the gently curving river. Ancient Indian camps are located here and there along the base of this unique and colorful mountain area. Numerous caves and sculpted boulders in weird erosional shapes litter the valley.[6]

Tuff formations are composed of volcanic ashes deposited after the eruptions that formed the Rocky Mountans. Ashes blanketed the Southwest, water erosion created valleys, canyons, and depressions.

Flooding water washed the ashes into these depressions, where they were saturated with lime and other minerals to form the cemented material called "tuff." Continued erosion formed them into their present natural formations. Some would call the area "badlands." That is because they have not yet turned loose of the idea that there must be trees, grass, and flowers to have beauty (Figs. 9.6 and 9.7).

Late in the evening the colors changed by a setting sun are a rich flame color, and above that flaming mass a full moon's cold light will provide all the drama of a color symphony one person can stand.

Interesting photo stops are found at Colorado Canyon put-in, Big Hill, and the Tepee roadside park (the take-out for the Colorado Canyon river trip). Big Hill has a 15 percent grade, which is the steepest allowed in Texas, and at the top is an excellent place to stop for photos. Several movies have been filmed in this area. The Contrabando movie set site and the spectacular geology in this area are also worth a stop.

Passage along the river was quite difficult for Lieutenants Whiting and Smith on their military reconnaisance to locate a new road for the pioneers crossing West Texas in 1849. The difficult passage in this area obviously led to the negative report when he returned to Washington.

9.7. One of my favorite formations is Penguin Rocks. If the light is just right, it looks as if a giant head is yawning.

9.8. The village of Shafter on US 67 south of Marfa is a pleasant stop for any visitor. The picturesque ruins and occupied buildings offer opportunities for a photo essay.

The government's final decision to choose a route through the Davis Mountains to the north is understandable.

At Lajitas you can arrange for raft trips down the Rio Grande, enjoy horseback rides or pack trips into the mountains, and explore Big Bend's canyons and desert. At Lajitas, swimming, golf, and tennis are also available. With an abundance of water, in short supply elsewhere, Lajitas can supply recreational activities not available in the national park.

If you intend to return to Marfa, the shortest route would be via Presidio. Backtrack to Presidio and turn north on US 67. You will notice the Chinati Mountains to the west as you approach Shafter.

Shafter is the location of a rich silver mine which has not been worked for many years. The mine operated for about sixty years and was the largest producer of silver in Texas. Today, most of Shafter lies in picturesque ruins. For years, the "ghost town" has been attractive to photographers, who spend hours wandering around with their cameras "at the ready." If you have not visited or explored this area with your camera, you should.

This town is also used by movie production crews. Shafter's abandoned church, for example, figured prominently in the movie *The Andromeda Strain* (Fig. 9.8).

Ever since pioneer Milton Faver built his three fortlike manors—Cíbolo, Ciénega, and Morita—in the vicinity of Shafter and planted his peach trees, it has been an important stop for travelers between Presidio del Norte and Marfa. Faver was known as the first "cattle king" in the area. According to local historians, he brought longhorn cattle across the Rio Grande from northern Mexico and, after branding them, turned them out to fend for themselves.[7]

Beginning in the 1880's, Shafter's main attraction was Don Milton Faver's peach brandy. It soothed dusty freighters and weary traders hauling goods between Marfa and Presidio. Faver's secure forts were also a sanctuary from Indians who made periodic raids on the ranches. The surrounding area is still the location of several peach orchards and many large ranches that, in the colorful words of historian E. E. Townsend, "lay scattered out like drying saddle-blankets."

10

WILD AND SCENIC RÍO

*P*ut all your worries under a flat rock and step into the tranquil beauty of the Big Bend Canyons of the Rio Grande.

Peter Koch

THE *Alpine Avalanche*, October 19, 1978, published a report we conservationists had been waiting to read for fifteen years. It announced that the Wild and Scenic Rivers Act would include about 190 miles of land bordering the Texas side of the Rio Grande. The area begins at the Chihuahua/Coahuila (Mexico) state line and continues downstream to the lines separating Terrell and Val Verde (Texas) counties.

Because we were too impatient to wait for spring, a small group of Texas Explorer Club members planned a sixty-nine-mile trip as soon as it could be arranged. We wanted to update our information about the river within Big Bend National Park, including the environment, recreational resources, and natural phenomena. We also wanted to map existing trails and possible routes to points of interest. Our trip began above Mariscal Canyon and continued downstream through Boquillas Canyon to the Adams ranch, completing the Big Bend National Park section of the river (Fig. 10.1).

A few weeks after the announcement, on a glorious November morning, five canoes were slipped into the emerald green water of the Rio Grande at the historic Talley ranch. A leisurely four-mile run took us into Mariscal Canyon and its spectacular twelve hundred–foot sheer

10.1. In 1978, the Texas Explorer Club surveyed Mariscal Canyon for existing trails and points of interest in the newly designated Wild and Scenic River section of the Rio Grande.

wall cliffs in time for a lunch and picture stop [Map 2]. After numerous hot and sultry side trips gathering information, we made camp inside the canyon.

During the night, a "norther" blew in. A blizzard began just before daybreak. It was Mariscal's first snow in twenty years. It covered the ground quickly and made morning chores a problem. Everyone was more interested in taking snow pictures than wading into the cold river, but at 11:00 AM we finally broke camp and were once again on our way.

We faced a strong wind loaded with snow and sleet, which chilled us to the bone. Temperatures stayed just above freezing for the rest of an extremely long and tiring day. That night we found shelter in the seclusion of a small canyon below the Solís place. Several fishermen also caught by the storm offered our group hot coffee and a pleasant evening around their campfire.

The next morning was clear and cold with ice water in our canteens, but toward noon the sun began to shine. We explored several ancient Indian campsites and guessed at the possible meaning of petroglyphs chipped on the boulders by ancient people who had once called this canyon their home.

A group of us made an interesting find at the caves on the eastern scarp about halfway up Mariscal Mountain. Someone thought we might find a treasure of Spanish silver hidden there. We did have a surprise waiting for us, but it was not Spanish treasure.

When we entered the cave, bats—thousands of bats—aroused by our presence startled us with their erratic flight. The floor of the cave was almost knee-deep in bat guano, and the heavy odor of nitrogen was stifling. The cave contained a single room measuring about one hundred feet deep, which pinched down to a size that was impassable.

I later learned that years ago the cave was routinely exploited for its guano treasure. There was a burro trail about a hundred feet below the cave. The guano, which is very light, was packed in burlap sacks and tossed down the cliff to the trail. Later, the sacks were picked up and loaded onto burros. The guano was used as fertilizer, probably in the Castolon area, where there was extensive irrigation farming at the time. Bat guano is a source of potassium nitrate, or saltpeter, a natural fertilizer.

I also learned the Mariscal Mountain caves were at one time scientifically explored for the presence of vampire bats. None were found, although they do occur less than a hundred miles to the south.

There is supposed to be another cave in the area located somewhere near the river. The cave entrance leads into a narrow passage which passes under the Rio Grande to an exit in Mexico. My search for that cave has been in vain.

Unlike in Santa Elena, there are several trails out of Mariscal Canyon. The one I recommend for hikers is near a grassy shelf on the U.S. side where a secondary canyon bisects the Rio Grande. From the shelf there is a trail on the canyon's right-hand slope. Be careful if you scramble along the edge of the rimrock for a better view. The limestone rock is treacherous, and a thousand-foot high dive into the Rio Grande would make the efforts of Acapulco's cliff divers look like a plunge into a kiddie pool.

The well-drained shelf provides ample space for overnight camping—but no firewood. The side canyon on the U.S. side leads to the top of the rimrock overlooking the river. From your camp, look for a trail on the right-hand slope of the canyon. Continue on this trail and bear to the left as you reach the summit. You should find an old river riders' trail. Follow it to the left, or west. It leads back to the Talley place (the canyon put-in) some five or six miles upstream. Another good reason for climbing the trail is the magnificent view from the top of the thousand-foot canyon gorge.

On Mariscal Canyon's Mexican side you might see a wax camp in operation. It takes about one hundred pounds of candelilla weed to make one pound of wax. At the time of our trip, I think it was worth about thirty-five cents a pound to the workers. Pictures of the work and burros are wonderful photos, but do not promise to send copies to the men unless you intend to follow through (Fig. 10.2).

Downriver from the wax camp, a trail leads to San Vicente. It's a difficult climb, but the rugged scenery toward the U.S. side of the canyon is worth the effort.

Below Mariscal Canyon is the relatively short San Vicente Canyon with colorful cliffs rising eight hundred feet. Here the Rio Grande is a placid stream and remains so through Hot Springs Canyon, still farther downstream. In the vicinity of Hot Springs, you can see the hot mineral waters gush from fissures in the limestone formations. Indians camped here too, judging from the numerous grinder holes along the riverbank.

Float trips through the canyons are usually made in small inflatable rafts, canoes, or kayaks, because of their maneuverability. Experienced canoeists find they can paddle upstream during normal water levels and

10.2. Wax camps are often found inside the canyons due to the availability of water and the cool environment. The bundles of candelilla wax on which the workers are sitting will be cooked for the important vegetable wax this plant yields.

return to their starting point, where their car may be parked, but it is better to paddle upstream and return downstream, in case sudden flood-water makes it impossible to paddle against the current. The old time-tested two-car system, one at each end, is still the best plan, with a downstream run all the way.

Many canyon runners, after a trip or two, find more to do than enjoy the relaxed float or the excitement of occasional rapids. Exploring side canyons and hiking trails to unknown, unmapped destinations may lead you to interesting and long-abandoned cave dwellings and unique experiences.

The last canyon on this particular journey was Boquillas, which is the largest and longest of the Big Bend National Park canyons (Fig. 10.3).

Exploration of Boquillas Canyon usually begins at the upstream portal below Rio Grande Village and continues to the Adams ranch at Stillwell Crossing. Most would agree this segment of the Rio Grande is perfectly suited for leisurely exploration in canoes or rafts. As in other park canyons, the Boquillas shoreline has been thoroughly explored wherever access is possible. Three important trails on the U.S. side lead from the river into the Deadhorse Mountains. Possession and examination of a topographical map is essential before attempting any of the Deadhorse Mountain backcountry trails.

About five miles into Boquillas Canyon we stopped at the candelilla wax camp located opposite the path to the canyon rim and the Marufo Vega trail. The Vega trail leads to an old river riders' camp, and from there it is possible to follow the Arroyo Venado to the point where the Strawhouse trail crosses the arroyo. [These trails are shown on the topographical map—Ed.]

On the slopes near the bluff there is a good campsite. From that location you will enjoy an amazing view of the Sierra del Carmen. The highlight of your Big Bend experience could be photographing the changing spectrum of reds reflected from the Sierra del Carmen escarpment at sunset. If you are fortunate enough to be camping there during the full moon, you will find the ethereal color values unbelievable.

10.3. The Emory Survey of the U.S./Mexico boundary crossed into Mexico to avoid Boquillas Canyon. A survey formation remains at the base of the Sierra del Carmen. Trips from Boquillas to Langtry were popular excursions for the Sierra Club.

After leaving Big Bend National Park, the river enters an incredibly remote and scenic lower canyon section of eighty-plus miles to the take-out near Langtry. Many hardy adventurers canoe from Boquillas through the lower canyons to Langtry each year. They enjoy the thrill of difficult white water at Reagan Canyon and Upper and Lower Madison Falls.

The isolation of this area is rarely found in developed America. If you decide to try this section of the river, take the advice of the Park Service, which warns that from Boquillas to Langtry you must be well prepared. There are no facilities, and access is limited due to rough terrain and constraints of private land. Because of the remoteness of the area, help may be many hours or days away. Extensive experience and preparation is absolutely essential. Permits and further information should be obtained from Big Bend National Park or local float-trip companies.

In 1901, Robert T. Hill of the U.S. Geological Survey wrote in *Century Magazine* of his 1899 trip through the lower canyons. His narrative is filled with admiration of the scenery but is extremely sketchy in the area of useful float information. I knew of no one who had run the lower canyons until Bill Thompson, a photographer and member of the Texas Explorers Club, made a three-month run down the Rio Grande from Presidio to the Gulf of Mexico in 1963. The following summer, Johnnie Beard of Odessa made the same trip.

Guy Skiles and his son Jack of Langtry were probably the first to take adventurous friends through the lower canyons' numerous rapids to the isolation of massive sheer wall canyons. One of their early passengers was Henry B. DuPont of Delaware, who came to the Big Bend frequently in the 1950's to "get away from it all." His photographs were used to illustrate the Langford book on Hot Springs published by the University of Texas Press. DuPont frequently expressed the opinion that the lower canyons were more exciting than the park canyons.

DuPont's reports encouraged Bob Burleson of Temple, Texas, to plan a thorough exploration of the canyons in 1965. Burleson more than anyone else called attention to the rare wilderness value set in an area of deep isolation.

The purpose of many Texas Explorers Club and Sierra Club trips in the sixties and seventies was to explore these canyons and support the upcoming Wilderness Bill. From their reports the lower canyons gained

an enthusiastic following, and the Big Bend area was finally included in
the Wild and Scenic Rivers legislation in 1978.

Another landmark adventure occurred on a canyon trip with U.S.
Supreme Court Justice William O. Douglas and a group of prominent
Texas writers and outdoorsmen who rafted Boquillas Canyon in 1965.
Discussing our environmental and esthetic values around the campfire
gave everyone new impressions to consider. Justice Douglas displayed
great sensitivity to the wilderness areas. He felt isolation and challenge
such as this would be therapeutic for many trying to find relief from
personal stress and urban crises.

Those of us who explored and experienced canyon trips in the early
days of the park found great satisfaction in this accomplishment, but
there was also the joy of having had an unforgettable adventure and the
companionship of sportsmen dedicated to preserving a Texas wilderness
for future generations.

I recall another organized float trip that was not so perfect. This trip was
through Santa Elena Canyon following several days of slow rain. Camp
was made at the Rock Slide after a dreary day on the river. All night we
heard the crashing of rocks falling from the canyon walls. It was a long
night as we lay awake, fearful that the next one would land on a bedroll.
Several chunks fell close by, cratering into the sandy soil, but we were
lucky (Fig. 10.4).

Rock fall is another reminder of the transformation occurring in the
Big Bend. Valleys and canyons are being dredged deeper by torrents of
water which fall during our summer rainy season. The Rio Grande, into
which all tributaries pour their runoff, has been called the "Great Excavator." After every rain, tons of rocks, boulders, sand, and mud are
carried by floodwater eventually to settle at the bottom of the Gulf of
Mexico.

Occasionally, a rumble and the roar of an avalanche announced the
breaking off of huge chunks from the face of the Sierra del Carmen
escarpment. Within the Chisos Mountain Basin a similar sloughing
from the igneous face of the cliffs adds to the talus slopes and scree
above the larger boulders that land below on a stabilized shelf or valley.

Santa Elena Canyon, with its hard thousand-foot cliffs of limestone,
seems solid enough to resist such erosion. But thousands of people float-

10.4. A member of the Texas Explorer Club enjoys a quiet float through Santa Elena Canyon.

ing the canyons have seen the Rock Slide—the great "barrier" in Santa Elena Canyon—and the house-sized boulders littering the bed of the river.

If you have not already done so, walk the trail from the portal up into Santa Elena Canyon to the large boulder at the river's edge. There you can feel the impact of the towering canyon walls. A photo of the canyon walls framing the vastness of the desert, with the Chisos Mountains on the distant horizon, is an excellent way to portray the canyon if you are unable to take one of the guided river trips.

The *Houston Chronicle's Texas Magazine* reported that an entirely new cadre of pioneer explorers had studied the Big Bend in April 1964. Sixteen of NASA's spacemen arrived to examine the geologic history of the Big Bend. Their instruction was designed to help them select moon rock samples after their arrival on the lunar surface. Among the students in the Big Bend desert were Richard F. Gordon Jr., Russell L. Schweickart, and Gordon Cooper. The astronauts' course covered such geologic features as faulting, folding, and other features that might be important in determining the origin and history of the moon. Particular interest was given the strata of the Santa Elena Canyon walls.[1]

Gutzon Borglum, who lived in San Antonio at the time, visited Big Bend in 1935 as the guest of his friend, local photographer W. D. Smithers. Borglum was the world-famous sculptor who designed and carved the Mount Rushmore presidential faces in South Dakota. While in Alpine, Borglum and his son talked with residents and presented a program at Sul Ross on the Mount Rushmore project.

At Johnson's ranch, Borglum had the opportunity to talk with Everett Townsend, considered the father of Big Bend National Park, and Roger Toll, of the National Park Service in Washington, DC. Under discussion was a proposal for carving huge heads of appropriate famous people on the Santa Elena Canyon walls. Thankfully, the idea never did reach the drawing board.

Borglum enjoyed the Big Bend and found the mountains, canyons, and even the petrified trees intriguing. Smithers said Borglum thought "all stone was potential sculpture."

What lies on top of Santa Elena's fifteen hundred–foot precipice remains a mystery except to a few hikers who have found the trail ascending the Mesa de Anguila near Lajitas. For many years, this trail led to a *tinaja* (a natural rock water hole) where a hunting camp and wax camp are located, not far from the edge of the cliff. The Rio Grande seen below the wax camp is but a tiny ribbon of water.

The tops of most mesas are relatively flat; however, Mesa de Anguila is exceedingly rugged and deeply cut by numerous canyons. Without the existing trail to the *tinaja*, a cross-country hike would be an ordeal made more severe by the absence of water on the mesa. The sound of water gushing over rapids in the river far below would make the torment even worse.

There must be a promontory there, overlooking the chasm of the river, from which a great photo could be made. I have yet to find it but did locate a sheltered nook where it was evident a live stream had once cascaded from the mesa into the river far below. What a picture that would have been.

In 1975, a group of Outward Bound rock climbers, accompanied by Dr. Dwight Deal of the Chihuahuan Desert Research Institute, proved that rock climbers with expertise could descend into beautiful Fern Canyon from the Sierra Ponce mesa.

One reason for the increasing popularity of the Rio Grande is its cleanliness. The river's shorelines are immaculate, free of industrial waste and commercial development. We experience an exhilarating sense of relaxation when we reach the end of a mountain trail or a riverbank of rippling, clean water. Let's keep it that way! When you are in tune with nature—in places like this—you too can forget life's problems and enjoy an unspoiled, rugged land.

Amerindians who followed game trails along watercourses and crossed from one stream to another were looking for food. European explorers followed those Indian trails looking for easy access to new opportunities in the Southwest. Today, we travel the Big Bend Country on a variety of trails, both old and new, as we search for a better understanding of the land, its creatures, and all growing things.

11

SILENCE OF THE DESERT

The deer and the antelope walk with each step gently
    placed.
Indians placed their soft-soled moccasins
silently upon the earth.
We should do no less today.

                                          Peter Koch

YEARS AGO, the Park Service issued me a permit to camp overnight at Tornillo Creek near the Black Peaks. It was twilight when I sat down on a huge fossilized tree stump. My bedroll was ready to crawl into, but there was time before dark to look around. A Texas tarantula wandered by, high off the ground on his spidery black legs. As the harmless creature passed he may have wondered what I was doing in such a lonely place.

I was there to watch the Comanche moon—the full moon of September—rise above the Deadhorse Mountains. I wanted to feel the presence of the Comanches, "Lords of the Great Plains," and their raiding parties, which passed this way each September on forays deep into Mexico to plunder the *rancherías* for slaves, goods, and livestock.

I wanted to imagine the sounds the camel expeditions of 1859 and 1860 made as they stopped here to allow their camels and mules to graze the waist-high grass, which Lieutenant Echols reported as the best they had seen.

I also felt a kinship with the early-day explorers and wanted to walk in the footsteps of conquistadors, padres, smugglers, soldiers, and traveling merchants who had camped in this place before me.

I also wanted to express my admiration for the prehistoric people. They were a patient people, courageous enough to venture into the

11.1. In the Big Bend–Davis Mountains are many spectacular landmarks near which archeologists have found evidence of where Stone Age hunters and food gatherers settled and maintained seasonal camps.

desplobado [unpopulated area] ages ago in search of food and water and a better life.

But most of all, I wanted to honor the memory of settlers I'd met who raised cattle, sheep, or goats, or who planted their bean fields at places much like this.

Often, as I listened to the old-timers speak of their experiences in the Big Bend, I knew that no matter how much I learn and share about this rugged land, no matter how many years I live in the Big Bend, I can never belong to the environment as completely as those who are natives of the Big Bend Country.

This spot on the creek bank near McKinney Hills was a likely place for the trail Echols, the camels, the Comanches, and others followed. The trail is eroded beyond identification, but they no doubt followed the easiest grades and contours of the land, and my campsite was not far off course (Figs. 11.1–11.3).

After a blazing sunset, the wind ceased and small sounds became audible in the growing silence. The sounds made by insects were the first to reach my ears, then the quiet calls of several desert birds. A great

11.2 and 11.3. Could these dim trails near the McKinney Hills have been used by the Comanches or Lieutenant Echols and the camels?

horned owl hooted mournfully from the direction of Black Peaks. A dozen bats cruised overhead, darting erratically in their chase for insects. The moon appeared like a shining metallic plate and—because of its brilliance—the stars winked then disappeared.

Soon after I crawled into my bedroll, the symphony of the night began. It was difficult to tell exactly where the coyotes' chorus was coming from, but what howling, yodeling, and yipping ensued! I listened for half an hour until they moved away like wild, wandering minstrels into a distant arroyo. It was very still.

As I lay there thinking of the courageous people who had preceded me, I wondered what Echols and the camel handlers would say if they could see the paved road that now crosses the fifty-seven deep arroyos that caused them so much grief.

What about the isolated pioneer ranchers who built their homes rock by rock and went to town but twice a year in mule-drawn wagons? What would they think of a ranch house with television, telephones, and indoor plumbing?

What would the Chisos Apaches do if they could ride their ponies into the Basin concessions area and find it active with automobiles, cabins, a public dining room, and curio shop? They would not recognize the area where once they huddled by meager campfires in a vain attempt to protect themselves from military annihilation.

And finally I thought about prehistoric days in which ancient man sought shelter and food in this silent land. How different our modern existence is compared to his daily life. The effort it takes to supply our needs is a mere nothing, and always present for us is "choice."

Stone Age man left a record of his life in several places near Black Peaks. He did not leave spears, darts, or arrowheads. The artifacts I saw were a fist ax and crude choppers and scrapers of a much earlier era. Those primitives had no choice. Think how severe their penalty was for one miscalculation.

There are times, while hiking the ancient trails and looking out over the vast country, when I wonder how long I could endure primitive conditions without the help of others. Could I, like the prehistoric Indians seen by Cabeza de Vaca, survive by following the ripening fruit? Could I throw myself bodily upon my enemies to preserve my life until tomorrow—perhaps only until tomorrow?

Could you?

Thirty-five years of my life were centered around promotional activities urging visitors to come to the Big Bend Country. My challenge was always how to plan new methods of attracting people to the natural world. As a conservationist in the 1960's, I echoed the thoughts of environmentalists who clearly stated, "We cannot revolt against pristine nature just because it lies unused for economic gain."

I joined the Big Bend Natural History Association when it was created in 1956. The purpose of this organization was, and still is, to serve and educate tourists. But an informational newspaper or brochure is not a substitute for experience. I believe knowledge and appreciation come from actually walking the trails, climbing the mountains, seeing the unusual flora and fauna, and taking time to understand the fragile relationship of one to the other. But is that enough?

We can look at our country and see how Anglo settlement changed the land. Unknowing pioneers in the Plains states plowed sensitive acreage and planted crops that could not grow for lack of rain. Their contribution to the West was watching the topsoil blow away.

In our own area, the problem was different. To produce mercury, the mine owners had to find wood to keep the retorts and furnaces in operation twenty-four hours a day—for years—until the nearby mountains and valleys were denuded. Historians tell us burro trains leading as many as fifty miles into remote mountains and valleys on both sides of the Rio Grande were a common sight along the trails.

Within five years, the mountains were stripped bare of trees. Monsoon rains which followed wreaked havoc on land that will spend centuries trying to recover.[1]

Hundreds of desert roses—hundreds—were scattered on a cuesta in the western portion of the park. By 1976, I failed to find a single specimen to photograph after an hour-long search. A mile on each side of any road in the park was gleaned of all rare plants by the mid-1970's. Fossil wood, rare cactuses, seashells, and gemstones were carried away by the truckload. My photos of the *pelicipods* lying on the desert floor may be the only proof that they were ever there (Fig. 11.4).

As erosion reveals more clues to our prehistoric human past, scavengers, souvenir hunters, and those with selfish interests will continue pocketing the history of the park, thinking only of their self-interested "wants."

Some don't bother to think at all! Abandoned houses, especially those with space beneath a wooden floor, are attractive to rattlesnakes. I heard of one group that chose to spend the night at the abandoned Wil-

11.4. These perfect specimens of Big Bend pelicipods *had been lying on their reef for more than thirty million years. They did not survive the first thirty-three years of protection in Big Bend National Park.*

son ranch house at Oak Creek. They escaped the serious consequences of snakebite as they slept in their bedrolls on the hardwood floor—just inches above a rattlesnake den.

I watched another group as they tugged at a beautifully weathered board. They stood beside an eight-foot rock wall which depended on the support of that board and narrowly escaped being covered by the rubble when it fell—along with a portion of the overhanging roof.

Youngsters playing on the ruined walls of the flood-damaged bathhouse at Hot Springs fell into the concrete tubs when they lost their balance because of loose flagstones. Because of incidents like these, many historic structures had to be razed by Park Service personnel in 1955, since it is their responsibility to protect visitors.

The spacious view from the South Rim is an important scenic feature. To the south, nearly a hundred miles away, is the lovely symmetry of Mexico's Sierra Encantada. Seventy-five miles away are the castellated towers of the Fronteriza Mountains. Just beyond the Rio Grande, the colorful cliffs of the Sierra del Carmen form a backdrop to the picturesque village of Boquillas.

Visitors are told that the view from the South Rim is like standing at the edge of the world. Unfortunately, there are times when visibility is so poor, due to air pollution, that none of these mountain ranges can be seen. It is not a daily event, but the degeneration of air quality and visibility are major concerns in all of the national parks.[2]

Water quantity and quality in some areas has deteriorated. Many springs have dried up or slowed to a trickle as the water table sinks. The Rio Grande—that "Brave River of the North"—flows more slowly due to the invasion of exotic plants like the salt cedar (tamarisk). This ornamental nonnative plant hogs light, space, and nutrients. A single tree can drink 150 gallons of water per day, thereby causing springs to disappear.[3]

Mankind has chosen other needs that supersede environmental concerns. Many predatory creatures—panther, bear, golden eagle—were destroyed during the pre-park ranching days when times were hard and knowledge was less valuable than livelihood. The animals' slow, tentative return from the mountains in Mexico has been controversial, but it will continue.[4]

Through the years, I discussed the damage being done to our scenic parklands with Ansel Adams and other prominent naturalists and conservationists, who have battled the same personal dilemmas. We photograph or write of the beauty to attract more people to the rare scenic wonders within our parks. But do our photography and writing indirectly contribute to the senseless destruction of the parks' environment? How can I continue to point out the Big Bend's marvelous wonders without encouraging more theft and vandalism?

My thoughts drift to the changes brought about by Nature. Sometimes we forget that Nature is never capricious.

A good example of this occurred in the 1940's, when Green Gulch was an overgrazed and much-abused valley. Only a few crooked piñon pines survived the ranchers' tree cutting for needed fence posts. Once the piñons were gone, small thickets of gnarled oaks took over the valley. Lechuguilla patches grew increasingly larger in the bare rocks. For a time, the gulch was not a pretty place.

An amazing change occurred during the drought of the 1950's. Dust storms caused the oaks in Green Gulch to die as winds delivered brown clouds of rich topsoil. The dirt was caught by the lechuguilla plants and trapped under rocks and gravel. It provided enough soil for seeds to germinate and produce a stand of grass, weeds, and small shrubs. The grasses gradually crowded out much of the lechuguilla. A few years later, a phenomenal new growth of piñon seedlings was noticed.

The piñon pines' regeneration was sensational. Naturalists from the regional Park Service office could scarcely believe that recovery, estimated to take fifty to one hundred years, was achieved in ten. The return of the piñon gave a proud new image to Green Gulch.

On the other hand, how about the creatures that depend on the acorn crop? Will they develop a taste for piñon nuts? It made me aware that perhaps Nature has a better plan for the Big Bend than those of us who struggle to control it by our own efforts.

I often recall the lesson I learned with Barton Warnock's hand lens and recall that the understanding I searched for in Santa Elena Canyon was not complete until I had explored each part of the Big Bend. As I continue to praise the Big Bend Country, I must consider my words carefully lest they inspire those who could innocently or purposefully destroy it by their actions.

After my night near the Black Peaks on Tornillo Creek, I woke to another coyote serenade. I rolled up my sleeping bag as I planned my day on the desert. The sunrise sky promised a beautiful day. I hoped that by afternoon massive thunderheads would appear. The desert sky is easier to look at when it is filled with clouds, thunderheads, shafts of rain, lightning. Sunsets, moonlight, and curling fingers of mist add impressions to the landscape that thrill me. When interesting clouds billow upward to decorate a rich blue sky, I also feel uplifted and, like a young newspaper photographer, am eager to point my camera where the action is.

After more than thirty-five years of photographing the natural history of the Big Bend Country, I often recall my anticipation when I first stepped out upon the desert. I relish those days of 1945 and the moments in my life when I explored the canyons, climbed the high mountain peaks, or stood on the desert sands and felt at peace.

We who love this country find joy and inspiration not only in a sunset sky but also in smelling the aroma of creosote after a rain, or the warm, muddy smell of the Rio Grande at flood stage. We are the ones who find cheer in the song of a canyon wren and never tire of the fiery afterglow of a sunset on the Sierra del Carmen.

It is time for each of us to dedicate ourselves—in any way we can— to teaching our children the joy and benefit of protecting the land. Our positive attitude will help the Big Bend Country remain a wondrous pleasure to be enjoyed by countless generations to come.

Notes

Introduction

1. Peterson and Fisher, *Wild America*, p. 212.
2. Douglas, *Farewell to Texas*, p. x.

Chapter 1

The columns in this chapter were published in the *Alpine Avalanche* in April and May 1975.

1. Lt. N. Michler, Corps Topographical Engineers, U.S.A., 1852. The description of the group's flood experience in a "Big Bend cañon" in 1852 is found in the Wm. H. Emory Report, vols. 1–10, chap. 5, quotations on pp. 91–92.
2. Hill, "Running the Canyons," pp. 371–387.
3. Ross Maxwell estimated the pile of rocks at the Rock Slide as 250 feet high and a quarter of a mile long. See *Guide Book 7*, p. 89.

Chapter 2

The columns in this chapter were published in the *Alpine Avalanche* between January 1976 and February 1980.

1. These small white-tailed deer, called the Carmen Mountain whitetail, or flagtail, are found only above four thousand feet in the Chisos Mountains and the Sierra del Carmen, which border the Rio Grande.
2. Jameson, *Story of Big Bend National Park*, pp. 38–43.
3. The original store built by the CCC was torn down some years ago. A flagstone patio and memorial to the men of the CCC now occupies the site. It is found just below the lodge and gift shop.
4. Byron Smith interview.

Chapter 3

The columns in this chapter were published in the *Alpine Avalanche* between May 1975 and June 1977.

1. U.S. Congress, Senate, *Report of Lt. William H. C. Whiting's Reconnaissance*, pp. 4–7.

2. U.S. Congress, Senate, *Diary of Lt. Edward L. Hartz*. See also U.S. Congress, Senate, *Report of Reconnaissance Routes from San Antonio to El Paso*.

3. U.S. Congress, Senate, *Diary of Lt. William H. Echols*, from entries of July 2 and July 4, 1860.

4. Ibid., p. 47.

5. Scobee, *Old Fort Davis*, pp. 1–3. Barry Scobee was also interviewed (during the trip around the Scenic Loop in 1976) by Peter Koch for his *Avalanche* columns.

6. Scobee, *Old Fort Davis*, pp. 2–3. Historians differ on Espejo's route, but the journal kept by Luxán as they returned home includes descriptions of the Fort Davis area and the number of leagues they traveled between the Pecos and the Conchos rivers.

7. Peter Koch, "Scenic Loop Road Log," p. 18.

Chapter 4

The columns in this chapter were published in the *Alpine Avalanche* between May 1975 and March 1980.

1. Jimmie Cooper, "Margarita de la Rosa" and "'Bobcat' Carter," unpublished, ca. 1957, in possession of June Price. These include Mrs. Cooper's reminiscences. Used with the consent of her husband, Mr. William A. Cooper.

2. Burns, "Bobcat Carter," pp. 16–19, 46–49.

3. The Boquillas bar was displayed in Alpine's Museum of the Big Bend in 2000. Additional information concerning its history was provided by Mary Bridges of the museum on March 18, 2003. Since May 10, 2002, the border has been closed at all crossings not designated an "official point of entry." The only bridge with this designation in the Big Bend is at Presidio/Ojinaga. Be sure to check with park staff or Brewster County officials on current border crossing restrictions and regulations.

4. The historic Lajitas Trading Post is probably the oldest remaining original establishment in the area; however, it was sold in about 2000 and renovated extensively to meet the demands of new explorers in the Big Bend—tourists. The original adobe trading post could tell many stories of the people who lived along the river.

5. Madison, *The Big Bend Country*, p. 123.

6. Luna, "The Story of Gilberto Luna," p. 3a. Luna's article adds interesting details to the information found in Peter Koch's 1975 column about Gilberto Luna.

Chapter 5

The columns in this chapter were published in the *Alpine Avalanche* between May 1975 and November 1979.

1. Dobie, *The Longhorns*, p. 41.

2. Shipman, *Taming the Big Bend*, pp. 26–27, 116.

3. Gray, *Shades of the West*, p. 118. Ted Gray was awarded the Texas Ranch Trailblazer award in 1997. It is awarded each year to those who "have ridden the trails, punched the cattle, dreamed the dreams, and met the challenge for their lives. . . . Their success, in a lifetime pursuit of the cattle business, makes them worthy of consideration as role models for generations to come" (Jeannie Choate, *Alpine Avalanche*, August 21, 1997).

4. Since May 10, 2002, the border has been closed at all crossings between Del Rio and Presidio/Ojinaga, except at the port of entry at Presidio.

5. Smithers, *Chronicles of the Big Bend*, pp. 118–123.
6. I found the letter in the Johnson's ranch file, Archives of the Big Bend, Alpine, Texas.

Chapter 7

The columns in this chapter were published in the *Alpine Avalanche* between May 1975 and January 1980.

1. Langford, *Big Bend.* The Langford family witnessed a more elaborate rain dance at San Vicente in 1910. Other rain dance information may be found in Miles, *Stray Tales.* These books contain many details and excellent descriptions of the ceremony.
2. Gipson, *The Cow Killers*, p. 3.
3. "Dinomania," p. 10. See also *Dinosaurs, Pterosaurs, and Crocodiles.* An amazing prehistoric creature was found in the lower Big Bend in 1999. The desert hillside site revealed the seventy million–year–old neck bones of an adult *Alamosaurus* which once roamed the floodplains of the Big Bend. When alive, the long-necked, long-tailed creature probably measured more than seventy-five feet from "stem to stern." That is almost twice the size of a T-Rex. Two juveniles discovered in the same area are about half that size. The recovered neck vertebrae alone stretched a distance of twenty-seven feet. The skull and jaws of a fifty-foot-long crocodile have also been found in the Big Bend. The creature was so large a man could stand upright in its wide-open jaws. Several thirty-five million–year–old rhinoceroslike mammals—eight feet tall and about fourteen feet long—were found in the Big Bend grasslands. Instead of one central horn, this species had two, one on each side of the snout. The site was found by a New Mexico science teacher vacationing in the park. He, quite properly, notified the science department at Sul Ross so that the area could be investigated and protected.
4. Newcomb, *North American Indians*, pp. 133–134.

Chapter 8

The columns in this chapter were published in the *Alpine Avalanche* between April 1976 and April 1978.

1. Rickett, *Wild Flowers of the United States: Texas.*
2. Warnock, *Wildflowers of the Big Bend Country, Texas;* idem, *Wildflowers of the Guadalupe Mountains and the Sand Dune Country, Texas;* idem, *Wildflowers of the Davis Mountains and the Marathon Basin, Texas.*
3. Koch, "Koch's Country," p. 40.
4. Wauer, *Naturalist's Big Bend*, p. 29.

Chapter 9

The columns in this chapter were published in the *Alpine Avalanche* between June 1975 and December 1977.

1. Hill interviews.
2. Ibid.
3. U.S. Congress, Senate, Diary of Lt. William H. Echols, July 17, 1860, p. 45.
4. Ibid.
5. Evelyn Dorsey, Fort Leaton, in a talk to visitors, September 2000.

6. Many changes have been made in Presidio County since 1980. Probably the most important is the creation of the 337,000 acre Big Bend Ranch State Park. It was established in 1988 and covers most of the area north of FM 170, including the amazing geologic wonder El Solitario. Stop at the Fort Leaton State Historic Site or the Barton Warnock Environmental Education Center to get copies of the literature that is available and to arrange for park tours or camping permits.

7. Milton Faver's three ranches are now listed in the National Register of Historic Places. They have been fully restored. There are thirty-five rooms at Cibolo Creek Ranch now available for those who want to experience a first-class resort in the Big Bend Country.

Chapter 10

The columns in this chapter were published in the *Alpine Avalanche* between April 1975 and February 1980.

1. "Rocky Road to the Moon," pp. 16–17.

Chapter 11

The columns in this chapter were published in the *Alpine Avalanche* between February 1976 and March 1980.

1. Ragsdale, *Quicksilver*, pp. 44–61.
2. Manning, "Big Bend Skies," p. 5.
3. Sánchez, "Changes in a Changeless Land," p. 1.
4. "Keep Wildlife Wild," p. 6.

Annotated Bibliography

Austin, Mary. *The Land of Little Rain*. Albuquerque: University of New Mexico Press, 1974.

The Back Country. Big Bend National Park, Tex.: National Park Service, 1953–1954.

Burns, C. Ross. "Bobcat Carter." *The Sage* (Sul Ross State University) (1973): 16–19, 46–49.

Dearen, Patrick. *Crossing Rio Pecos*. Fort Worth: Texas Christian University, 1996.

Deckert, Frank. "Go to the River." In *Big Bend: Three Steps to the Sky*, p. 50. Big Bend National Park, Tex.: Big Bend Natural History Association and the National Park Service, 1981.

Dobie, J. Frank. *The Longhorns*. Boston, Mass.: Little, Brown, 1941.

Douglas, William O. *Farewell to Texas, a Vanishing Wilderness*. New York: McGraw-Hill, 1967.

Gard, Wayne. *The Chisholm Trail*. Albuquerque: University of New Mexico Press, 1954.

Gipson, Fred. *The Cow Killers: With the Aftosa Commission in Mexico*. Illus. Bill Leftwich. Austin: University of Texas Press, 1956.

Gray, Ted. *Shades of the West: A Cowboy's Memoirs*. Self-published, ca. 1980. A well-written description of a rancher's life and work.

Hill, R. T. "Running the Canyons of the Rio Grande." *Century Magazine* 61 (November 1900–April 1901): 371–387.

Jameson, John. *The Story of Big Bend National Park*. Austin: University of Texas Press, 1996.

"Keep Wildlife Wild." *Big Bend Paisano* 20, no. 3 (Winter 2002): 14.

Koch, Peter. "Exploring the Big Bend . . . with Peter Koch." *Alpine Avalanche*, columns, 1975–1980.

———. "Koch's Country." *Texas Parade* (March 1970): 40.

———. "Scenic Loop Road Log." In *Guide [to the] Big Bend—Davis Mountains*. Alpine, Tex.: *Alpine Avalanche*, June 11, 18, 25, 1964.

———. "Tips for Camera Toters." In *The Back Country*. Big Bend National Park, Tex.: National Park Service, 1953–1954.

Langford, J. Oscar, with Fred Gipson. *Big Bend: A Homesteader's Story.* Austin: University of Texas Press, 1952.

Luna, Demencio C., Jr. "The Story of Gilberto Luna." *Alpine Avalanche* (August 29, 1999).

Madison, Virginia. *The Big Bend Country.* Albuquerque: University of New Mexico Press, 1955.

Manning, Mary Kay. "Big Bend Skies." *Big Bend Paisano* 22, no. 3 (Winter 2002).

———. "Night Skies over the Big Bend." *Big Bend Paisano* 22, no. 3 (Winter 2002).

Maxwell, Helen. *A Guide for the Big Bend.* Photos Peter Koch. Self-published, 1950.

Maxwell, Ross. *Guide Book 7.* Austin: Bureau of Economic Geology, University of Texas, 1968.

McDonald Observatory. *A Self-guided Walking Tour of Mt. Locke and Mt. Fowlkes.* Austin: University of Texas at Austin, McDonald Observatory, n.d.

Miles, Elton. *Stray Tales of the Big Bend.* College Station: Texas A&M University Press, 1993.

Moore, Wayne. "Dinosaurs, Pterosaurs, and Crocodiles." Washington, D.C.: Division of Interpretation and Visitor Services, National Park Service, 1996.

Newcomb, W. W., Jr. *North American Indians: An Anthropological Perspective.* Pacific Palisades, Calif.: Goodyear, 1974.

Peterson, Roger Tory, and James Fisher. *Wild America.* Boston, Mass.: Houghton Mifflin, 1955.

Ragsdale, Kenneth Baxter. *Quicksilver: Terlingua and the Chisos Mining Company.* College Station: Texas A&M University Press, 1976.

———. *Wings over the Mexican Border.* Austin: University of Texas Press, 1984.

Rickett, Harold William. *Wild Flowers of the United States: Texas.* 2 vols. New York: McGraw-Hill, 1969–1970.

Sánchez, Gus. "Changes in a Changeless Land." *Big Bend Paisano* 21, no. 3 (Winter 2001).

———. "Rocky Road to the Moon Leads through Big Bend." *Houston Chronicle* (May 17, 1964).

Scobee, Barry. *Old Fort Davis.* San Antonio, Tex.: Naylor, 1947.

Shipman, Mrs. O. L. (Alice Jack). *Taming the Big Bend.* N.p., 1926.

Smithers, W. D. *Chronicles of the Big Bend.* Austin, Tex.: Madrona Press, 1977.

Vandenberg, Tom. "Dinomania." *Big Bend Paisano* (Winter 2001).

Warnock, Barton H. *Wildflowers of the Big Bend Country, Texas*. Photos Peter Koch. Alpine, Tex.: Sul Ross State University, 1970.

——. *Wildflowers of the Davis Mountains and Marathon Basin, Texas*. Photos Peter Koch. Alpine, Tex.: Sul Ross State University, 1977.

——. *Wildflowers of the Guadalupe Mountains and the Sand Dune Country, Texas*. Photos Peter Koch. Alpine, Tex.: Sul Ross State University, 1974.

Wauer, Roland H. *Naturalist's Big Bend*. College Station: Texas A&M University Press, 1992.

Government Documents

U.S. Congress. Senate. Diary of Lt. Edward L. Hartz to Maj. David H. Vinton. In *Report to the Secretary of War*. 36th Cong., 1st Sess., Sen. Exec. Doc. no. 2, 1859–1860. Serial 1024, pp. 422–441.

——. Diary of Lt. William H. Echols. In *Report of Reconnaissance West of Camp Hudson*. 36th Cong., 2nd Sess., 1860–1861. Serial 1079, pp. 36–50.

——. *Report of Lt. William H. C. Whiting's Reconnaissance of the Western Frontier of Texas*. 31st Cong., 1st Sess., Sen. Exec. Doc. no. 64, 1849–1850. Serial 562.

——. *Report of Reconnaissance West of Camp Hudson*. 36th Cong., 2nd Sess., 1860–1861. Serial 1079.

——. *Reports of Reconnaissance Routes from San Antonio to El Paso*. 31st Cong., 1st Sess., Sen. Exec. Doc. no. 64, 1849–1850, Serial 562.

Archives

Alpine Avalanche, Alpine, Texas.

Archives of the Big Bend, Sul Ross State University, Alpine, Texas. Nathan Twining, letter, 1958, from Twining to W. D. Smithers, regarding his memories of Johnson's field. In "Johnson's Ranch" file.

Interviews

Hill, Celia, and Rusty Hill. Ruidosa, Texas, June 3, September 27, 2000. Interviews with the author. How to build an ocotillo fence and a tire–aluminum can wall were just two of the things I learned from these lifelong residents of the Big Bend. Interesting environmental solutions, to be sure.

Smith, Byron. Hillsboro, Texas, 2000. Interview with and letter to author.

INDEX